# BEGINNING

# OLD

# TESTAMENT

# S T U D Y

# BEGINNING
# OLD
# TESTAMENT
## STUDY

JOHN ROGERSON

JOHN BARTON

DAVID J. A. CLINES

PAUL JOYCE

**Chalice Press**
St. Louis, Missouri

First published in 1998 in Great Britian by SPCK, Holy Trinity Church, Marylebone Rd., London NW1 4DU.

© Copyright 1998 by John Rogerson, David J.A. Clines, Paul Joyce, and John Barton. North American edition published 1998 by Chalice Press, P.O. Box 179, St. Louis, MO 63166-0179.

Cover design: Wendy Barnes

Cover art: *A Prophet Addressed by an Angel* (detail) by Sebastiano del Piombo,
Gift of Robert H. and Clarice Smith;
Photograph © Board of Trustees,
National Gallery of Art, Washington, D.C.

Art direction: Elizabeth Wright

This book is printed on acid-free, recycled paper.

Visit Chalice Press on the World Wide Web at
www.chalicepress.com

10  9  8  7  6  5  4  3  2  1          98  99  00  01  02          03

### Library of Congress Cataloging–in–Publication Data

Beginning Old Testament study / John Rogerson ... [et al.]
    p.  cm.
    Includes bibliographical references and index.
    ISBN 0-8272-0227-X
    1. Bible. O.T.—Criticism, interpretation, etc.  2. Bible. O.T.—Study and teaching.  I. Rogerson, J.W. (John William), 1935-  .
BS1192.B37  1998                98–37304
221.6'1—dc21                    CIP

Printed in the United States of America

# Contents

# The Contributors

JOHN ROGERSON is Emeritus Professor of Biblical Studies at the University of Sheffield. He taught from 1964 to 1979 at the University of Durham, and from 1979 to 1996 at Sheffield, where he was Head of the Department of Biblical Studies from 1979 to 1994. His many books covering aspects of the history, geography and sociology of ancient Israel, as well as the history of Old Testament criticism, include *Anthropology and the Old Testament* (1978), *Old Testament Criticism in the Nineteenth Century: England and Germany* (1984), *Atlas of the Bible* (1985), *The Old Testament World* (1989, with P.R. Davies), *Genesis 1–11* (1991) and *The Bible and Criticism in Victorian Britain* (1995).

JOHN BARTON has taught Old Testament at Oxford since 1974, and in 1991 was appointed to the Oriel and Laing Chair of Biblical Interpretation, and to a Professorial Fellowship at Oriel College. He is a leading expert in the fields of the theology and ethics of the Old Testament, and of its modern interpretation. His books include *Reading the Old Testament – Method in Biblical Study* (1984), *Oracles of God – Perceptions of ancient Prophecy in Israel after the Exile* (1986), *Biblical Interpretation* (1988, with R. Morgan), *The Spirit and the Letter* (1996), and *People of the Book* (1997, new edition).

DAVID J.A. CLINES has taught in Sheffield since 1964, and in 1985 was appointed to a personal Chair. He succeeded John Rogerson as Head of Department in 1994. A pioneer in the fields of literary and ideological criticism of the Bible, his many works include *The Theme of the Pentateuch* (1978), *Job 1–20* (1989), *What does Eve do to Help? And Other Readerly Questions to the Old Testament* (1990) and *Interested Parties – The Ideology of Writers and Readers of the Hebrew Bible* (1995).

PAUL JOYCE is University Lecturer in Old Testament at Oxford, and a Fellow of St. Peter's College. He taught previously at

Ripon College, Cuddesdon, and the University of Birmingham. One of his specialities is the Book of Ezekiel, on which he has completed a commentary, as well as his monograph *Divine Initiative and Human Response in Ezekiel* (1989).

# Preface to the Second Edition

It is nearly twenty years since two of the contributors to this volume discussed the desirability of producing an introduction to Old Testament studies that would bridge the gap between academic study and 'beginners'. There already existed standard works introducing the different books of the Old Testament, describing their content and offering scholarly opinions as to their date and authorship. What was lacking was a book for beginners that introduced them to methods and approaches that were taken for granted by scholars but rarely discussed. It was our feeling that ignorance of these methods opened up a cultural gap between beginners and scholars that made it difficult for beginners to have very much idea of what Old Testament scholarship was trying to achieve, and made the Old Testament component of college courses dull and difficult. The introduction to the first edition put it like this, addressing 'beginners' directly:

> The present book may be likened to a travel guide. Its purpose is to illumine the academic study of the OT, so that both the study, and the OT itself, are better appreciated. It aims to help you over some of the first hurdles rather than to tell you everything that you will need to know by the time you have completed your studies.

The outcome of the discussions was *Beginning Old Testament Study*, first published in 1983 and subsequently reprinted six times. The contributors have been well pleased with the success of the volume; but Old Testament studies is a fast-moving subject, and as time has gone on the contributors have become only too well aware of the need for the book to be revised. They are grateful to SPCK for their willingness to publish a revised edition.

One thing that has not changed since 1983 is the general ignorance of the content of the Old Testament on the part of students beginning courses at college level in Theology, Biblical

Studies or Religious Studies. For such students, the Old Testament is still an unknown text studied by unfamiliar methods, and in a way quite different from what may be familiar to those students who may have a church background. The need for a work such as *Beginning Old Testament Study* is therefore as pressing as it ever was. However, the changes in the academic study of the Old Testament since the appearance of the first edition have been considerable.

Although David Clines' contribution to the first edition on methods in Old Testament study was very forward looking in 1983 (the contributions were written in 1981–2), there was no mention in it of feminist or liberation or ideological criticism. Although it dealt extensively with literary methods, it did not mention deconstruction. Similarly, John Rogerson's essay on the world-view of the Old Testament concentrated upon insights from social anthropology but said little about sociology. There have also been enormous changes in the study of the history of ancient Israel, such that a radical school has emerged that questions whether very much can be known about ancient Israel's history before the Babylonian exile in 587 BCE. The very fact that most books now published on the Old Testament use BCE (before the Common Era) instead of BC (before Christ) reflects another change in Old Testament study, a change that has tried to be sensitive to Jewish communities and the fact that what Christians call the Old Testament is sacred scripture to believing Jews.

This sensitivity towards Jewish feelings has led many scholars, especially in North America, to abandon the term Old Testament altogether, and to substitute for it the term Hebrew Bible. Since the present volume retains the former term, a word is needed about this issue.

All the contributors to this second edition are sensitive about using the term Old Testament. The difficulty lies in finding a suitable alternative. 'Hebrew Bible' presents at least two problems. The first is that on an analogy with 'English Bible' or 'German Bible', the meaning of Hebrew Bible is most naturally the Bible in the Hebrew language. Now it would be splendid if all students of the Old Testament were in fact reading the texts only in Hebrew. Unfortunately, this is a privilege available only to a few among non-Jews. Second, the phrase Hebrew Bible obscures the fact that while the texts of the twenty-four books accepted as canonical by Jews and most Protestant Christians were originally written in Hebrew, access to these books in something approaching their original form is not simply via the Hebrew text as it has come down to us. Ancient translations in Greek, Latin and Syriac often retain readings that appear to be superior to what is found in the Hebrew as it has come down to us, so that the scholarly study of the Old Testament is not simply a study of texts in Hebrew. There is also the point that, for Catholic, Eastern, Oriental and some Protestant traditions within the Christian churches, the Old Testament is wider than the twenty-four books, including some that were not originally written in Hebrew.

If 'Hebrew Bible' is problematic, what alternatives are there? One possibility favoured by some is 'First Testament'; but whether this is really an improvement on Old Testament is a matter of opinion. At the heart of the matter is the fact that Old Testament is a Christian designation that appears to put it on an inferior footing to the New Testament and therefore to devalue it, a move that is felt to be insensitive to Jews. Not everyone will be convinced that First Testament avoids this implication. For the moment, it has to be admitted that a satisfactory alternative to Old Testament has not yet been suggested, which is why the present work retains Old Testament. The discussion is important, however, in helping scholars and students to be sensitive to the fact that what the churches have called the Old Testament is also the property of Judaism and Jews, and that the churches do not have a monopoly on it. It is also the case that Old Testament scholars would reject the idea that the Old Testament is somehow inferior to the New. As is pointed out in the Epilogue to the present volume, the Old Testament has much to say on matters of religious faith on which the New Testament is silent; and because of its much greater length and diversity, the Old Testament far outstrips the New Testament in its literary, cultural, social and dramatic dimensions. Some of these factors have been highlighted in the developments in Old Testament study since 1983.

It is the hope of the contributors, then, that this second edition will introduce a new generation of students young and old to the changed and changing nature of Old Testament study. If this second edition fulfils its aims as successfully as the original edition appeared to do, the contributors will be well satisfied.

# Introduction

On any showing, the Old Testament is a remarkable collection of books produced by a remarkable group of people. Except for several brief spells when they ruled over small neighbouring peoples, the ancient Israelites were not a military or political force to be reckoned with. They lived at the edge of the main international route from Egypt to northern Mesopotamia, and for much of their history they struggled to retain their identity in the face of the imperialistic expansions of Egypt, Assyria, Babylon, Persia, the Hellenistic successors of Alexander the Great, and Rome. On several occasions, they retained their separate identity at the expense of becoming vassal states. In 721 BCE, the Assyrians brought to an end the separate national existence of the ten tribes that had formed the northern kingdom since Solomon's death. In 587 BCE, the Babylonians brought to an end the southern kingdom of Judah. The temple in Jerusalem was destroyed, and the city itself was sacked. The most prominent of the people were taken off to exile in Babylon, there to join a larger number of exiles from Judah who had been deported on the occasion of the first great Babylonian victory in 597.

The loss of Jerusalem and of the temple in 587 ought to have brought to an end the separate existence of the ancient Israelites. They ought to have disappeared like their neighbours Ammon, Edom, Moab and the Philistines, leaving behind only traces that the archaeologists would discover 2,500 years later. But they did not cease to exist. Characteristically, a prophetic group among the exiles took up and enlarged the theme of the preaching of Jeremiah and Ezekiel at the time of Jerusalem's fall – that this fall was God's punishment of his people because of their persistent disloyalty. The exile became a time for positive reflection upon the past, and for the discovery of the value of suffering. The exiles looked forward in hope to a new beginning, a hope partially satisfied when, in 540, the Persian king Cyrus allowed some exiles to return to Jerusalem with a view to rebuilding the temple.

This remarkable story of a people that refused to die is told in the OT. But just as remarkable is the way in which it is told. It is true that the OT contains sections in which the achievements of the Israelites are proudly presented. The section in I Kings 3–10 about Solomon and all his glory springs readily to mind. But on the whole, the story of the ancient Israelites is told not in order to glorify their achievements, but rather to emphasize their persistent disloyalty to God. The record is highly critical, and few kings, for example, escape without censure. Even David, who came in later OT times to be regarded as a model king, is spared nothing as 2 Samuel 9–20 deals with his adultery with Bathsheba, his disposal of her husband, and the subsequent breakdown of relationships within his own family.

The criticism of Israel that runs through the Old Testament is an important clue to its origin and purpose. It is not the national literature of the ancient Israelite people. It is a collection of religious books, and it is probably the work of a smallish group who, generation after generation, bore witness to faith in God, often in the face of official disapproval, persecution, and even death.

One way of characterizing the OT is to describe it as the story of the struggle between the God of Israel and the God of the OT. The God of Israel was the god that the people wanted for their own convenience – a god who would win their battles, cure their illnesses, and look after their general well-being. After all, did not the old stories tell of how he had defeated the Egyptians and rescued the people from slavery? But this view of God was constantly challenged by those we may call the servants of the God of the OT. They proclaimed that Israel existed to be the servant of God, and not vice versa. They pointed out the injustices done to the poor and the defenceless. They denounced the attempts of rulers and people alike to confuse God with the gods of other peoples. They stressed the implications of their belief that God was the sovereign lord of heaven and earth, and that it was his purpose to bless all the nations by establishing his universal rule. Those who proclaimed thus, did so because their encounter with their God left them no option.

The story of Israel, told critically by those who proclaimed God's wider purposes for mankind, can be found in parts of the Pentateuch (Genesis–Deuteronomy) and above all in what are known as the former prophets (Joshua–2 Kings). The latter prophets (Isaiah–Malachi) provide a prophetic companion to that story. However, the OT contains much other material. In the books of Job and Ecclesiastes are to be found two of the most frank and penetrating explorations of the problems of suffering and doubt in any religious literature. The Psalms constitute a treasury of texts for use in worship, whether public or private, and frankly express the doubts, sufferings and anger of their authors, as well as great sentiments about faith and hope in God.

In many ways, the OT is a remarkably contemporary book. Its writers were familiar with the tides of war rolling across a continent first one way, then the other, as this century has seen on the continent of Europe. The future often seemed threatening. Starvation through famine or pestilence, death through epidemics, loss of livelihood, suffering and injustice were not unknown. The writers of the OT had no more reason for hoping in the victory of the purposes of God than we have today, yet they persisted in their hope, and they survived. Again, parallels can be drawn between the Church and Israel as the people of God. In a nominally Christian country, there is a struggle between the conventional or 'folk' religion of the majority, and a witness of the minority that sometimes brings them into conflict with the majority. The history of the Church shows it to have been in many ways as faithless to God as was ancient Israel, and constantly in need of prophetic renewal.

If the OT contains a remarkable story remarkably told, if it is frank about doubt and unjustified suffering, if it is a book of hope written from situations no more favourable to hope than our present world seems to be, it might be expected that OT courses would be among the most interesting and exciting in college and university curricula. Yet this does not seem to be the case. From many quarters the complaint is heard that students entering higher education come with very low expectations about the value of OT study, and that their attitude is not altered by their courses. Among the reasons for this may be ignorance of the content of the OT, something very noticeable in present-day students. For many years now, schools and even Sunday schools have given up any attempt to provide pupils with a knowledge of the content of the Bible. Even regular worshippers in the Church of England, the present writer's own church, will be lucky to hear an OT lesson regularly at the Parish Communion, and a sermon on the OT will be a rarity. The OT has become largely unknown, even to many worshippers.

But the fault does not lie entirely with schools and churches. In colleges and universities, we have taken too much for granted. We have confronted our students not only with an unfamiliar text, but with unfamiliar methods by which to study it. We have assumed too easily that students would appreciate the difference between the academic study of the OT and its use in worship and evangelism. We have overlooked the fact that almost all our students have a New Testament orientation, and that they look back to the OT as preparation, anticipation or background for the NT. OT teachers, on the other hand, often see the matter differently. For them, the OT can, and must, stand on its own feet. It is an expression arising from many concrete situations over many hundreds of years, of faith in the living God.

The essays that follow this introduction are not intended as a guide to the content of the OT, but rather as a guide to how to approach the academic study of the OT. The opening chapter provides a brief account of the history of OT study, so as to enable beginners to appreciate more readily the nature of academic as opposed to other approaches. The second chapter deals with the methods in OT study. For over two hundred years, scholars have investigated the possible sources used by the biblical writers, and the manner in which these sources were combined together. Yet it is the text as we have it that must always remain the basis of interpretation, and Chapter 2 provides guidelines both for interpreting Old Testament literature and for relating the various methods to this end.

There follows a chapter about the historical traditions in the OT. What is the purpose of these traditions, how do they compare with modern scholarly reconstructions of ancient Israel's history, and what happens if the modern scholar feels it necessary to 'correct' the account presented in the OT? Chapter 4 sketches some of the cultural differences between the OT world and the contemporary world. These differences are not so great that we can only understand the OT if we read it with a special kind of cultural spectacles. On the other hand, at some points we can appreciate it more readily if we make some cultural adjustments to our approach.

In the second half of the book there is a deliberate shift to some of the theological problems encountered in OT study. The chapters on OT theology and on ethics touch on some of the most difficult questions. For many people, the ethics of the OT are those of a primitive or barbaric tribe, while if the OT is to provide material for theology, it is at best a record of human search for God, small parts of which almost reflect the spirit of the NT. While not shirking the difficulties, our chapters seek a more positive approach, and try to dispel some of the popular 'myths' about the OT.

The same is true of the chapters about the individual and the community, and the relation of the OT to the NT. The first of these is concerned particularly with justice and punishment, and shows how the tension between individual responsibility and the corporate consequences of wrongdoing runs throughout the OT. The final chapter discusses and dismisses the view that the OT has no place in the Church, that the OT is about wrath and the NT is about love, and that we must interpret the OT today in the manner in which it was interpreted in NT times. An Epilogue discusses the contemporary use of the OT.

# 1

## An Outline of the History of Old Testament Study

### JOHN ROGERSON

Everyone is born into particular cultural and historical circum-stances. Children born in the mid-1980s are growing up in a world dominated by computer technology such that they are much more at home in this than their parents, and probably know more about computing than their teachers! When the contributors were writing the essays for the first edition of *Beginning Old Testa-ment Study,* very few scholars could afford the very rudimentary word processing packages that then existed. Today, the scholar who does not use a word processor is a rarity. All this is in great contrast to the generation that was growing up just before the Second World War. The computer had not yet been invented, and the international scene was dominated by the threat to the peace of Europe of the ambitions of Hitler's Germany. Today, the nations of Europe are engaged in the quest for greater unity and co-operation.

We have no control over the cultural and historical circum-stances in which we find ourselves before we reach adulthood; but we learn to live with them, and we come to terms with them. The same is true when you begin academic studies. You have no control over the burning issues and the favoured solutions that dominate a subject at the point in time when you begin your studies. Yet you have to come to terms with these burning issues and what are thought to be their most likely solutions.

There is, however, a difference between how we are affected by the general circumstances in which we grow up, and how we find an academic discipline when we enter it. We cannot easily escape from the general circumstances of life. In an age of saturation coverage of news, they are all too familiar. What has been happening in academic study is, however, quite unfamiliar to us. When we begin academic study, we may well be amazed at what the burning issues are. They may concern questions that we have never thought of and which we cannot even fully understand.

In the case of Old Testament study there is an additional difficulty. If we have any familiarity with the OT, we have almost certainly got it either from church or school. There is the possibility that we have learned to think about the OT in ways that will not be helpful for academic study. We may have been taught to accept everything the OT says at its face value, so that it will come as a shock to discover that academic study subjects the OT to close and critical scrutiny. Or we may have been taught that the OT is the record of human searching for God before the coming of Christ. As a result, we may find it hard to believe that the OT contains anything of permanent religious significance. We may also have learned some false ideas about the history of critical biblical scholarship. For example, we might think that critical scholarship is something essentially recent, perhaps the result of theologians giving in to scientists after the publication of Darwin's *Origin of Species* in 1859, whereas before the nineteenth century, Christian scholars were never concerned with critical questions.

In our ordinary lives, even a superficial study of the history of how circumstances have come to be as they are can help us to understand, and in some cases react positively to, the situation in which we find ourselves. This is also true with regard to academic study in general, and to OT study in particular. We may find it much easier to come to terms with critical scholarship if we know something about its history. The outline that will be presented in the remainder of this chapter will be highly selective. It will have the following aims. First, to show that in one sense of the word critical, OT scholarship has always been critical. Second, to try to show what was the really new factor that emerged with the historical–critical method in the late eighteenth century. Third, to attempt to place modern fundamentalism in the context of this brief historical sketch, and explain why clashes between fundamentalism and critical scholarship still occur.

## *Critical scholarship before the Reformation*

In I Samuel 13.1 the traditional Hebrew text literally translated reads: 'Saul was one year old when he began to reign, and he reigned two years over Israel.' The earliest translators and commentators on this passage could have said if they so wished, 'with God, all things are possible. It seems incredible that a man could become a king and commander at the age of one; but this is what the Scripture says, and we must accept it, lest we imply that God is a liar.' Perhaps some very early scholars did say this. What we know, however, is that there were scholars who realized that there was a difficulty. Not only did the verse contradict what is known about human growth and development; it contradicted other passages about the life of Saul in I Samuel. Thus the difficulty was solved in one of three ways. In the ancient Greek translations of the OT, the earliest of which goes back to pre-Christian times, the verse is either omitted entirely, or a figure such as thirty is given. Ancient Jewish interpretation, which is reflected in the Authorized Version of the Bible (1611), produced sense by doing violence to Hebrew usage. The AV has, 'Saul reigned one year; and when he had reigned two years over Israel, Saul chose him three thousand men . . .'. We have here good examples of critical scholarship. Faced with a passage that contradicted reason and the evidence of other passages, ways were found of getting sense out of the verse. Of the three solutions mentioned, the one nearest to the truth was probably that that assumed a number had been lost, and that provided it by guesswork.

A remarkable piece of critical scholarship in the early Christian centuries was concerned to help establish the correct text of the OT. The OT is sometimes quoted in the New Testament with significant differences from the text of the OT as we have it. A good example is the quotation of Amos 9.11–12 in Acts 15.16–18. Amos 9.12 reads (RSV):

> that they may possess the remnant of Edom and all the nations who are called by my name, says the LORD who does this.

Acts 15.17–18 cites the verse as follows:

> that the rest of men may seek the Lord, and all the Gentiles who are called by my name, says the Lord, who has made these things known from of old.

Such differences must have been worrying to early Christian scholars, quite apart from the fact that Jewish apologists accused Christians of falsifying the text of the OT, while Christians returned the accusation. In an attempt to provide the information on the basis of which the correct text of the OT could be established, Origen compiled his *Hexapla*.

Origen (185–245 CE) lived in Caesarea, and had a patron who provided him with ample secretarial assistance. The *Hexapla* was an edition of the OT in which the text was set out in six main parallel columns. The first column contained the Hebrew text, the second transliterated this into Greek, while the remaining columns contained translations of the OT into Greek. The work was over 6,000 pages long, and survived until the Moslem invasions of the seventh century. It is known today only from quotations in the works of scholars who consulted it.

Two examples of critical scholarship in the fourth century are provided by the work of Eusebius of Caesarea, and Jerome. Eusebius compiled an *Onomasticon*, which was an attempt to identify the places mentioned in the Bible. He drew upon the work of earlier writers, as well as on his own knowledge of the land of the Bible. Jerome, who lived in Bethlehem, was the greatest Christian Hebrew scholar in the early Church. At a time when there were no Hebrew grammars, dictionaries or concordances, he learned Hebrew from local Jews sufficiently well to enable him to translate the OT from Hebrew into Latin. He also wrote commentaries and treatises on the OT, and for many centuries his work provided Christian scholars in the West with most of their knowledge about the Hebrew of the OT.

The critical scholarship so far described has demonstrated the desire to establish so far as possible the most correct text of the OT, and the wish to gain mastery over the main language in which it was written. Early critical scholarship also faced up to questions that we might suppose were not discussed until modern scientific times. In *The City of God* (426 CE), Augustine of Hippo wrestled with the following questions, among others. Were the six days of creation described in Genesis I days such as we know them, or did the days stand for much longer periods? How was it that light was created three days before the creation of the sun and the moon? Before the Flood, we read in Genesis that people lived for hundreds of years, and that in some cases they did not begin to have children until they were over one hundred and fifty years old. Are we to understand these years as the same as our years, or could they have been much shorter? Were there really giants on the earth in the days before the Flood?

Augustine answered as follows. The days and the light

mentioned in Genesis I were different from what we understand by days and light. 'What kind of days these were it is extremely difficult, or perhaps impossible for us to conceive, and how much more to say!' (Book II, ch. 6). On the lengths of the lives of those who lived before the Flood, Augustine had no doubt that their years were the same as our years. It was obvious that the years mentioned in the account of the Flood had ordinary days and months like our years, and there was no reason to suppose that the years of Genesis 5 were any different from those of Genesis 6–9. That some ancestors did not seem to have produced children until they were over one hundred and fifty was a difficulty. Either they did not have children until that age because they matured very much more slowly; or they deliberately abstained from having children. Augustine allowed that people before the Flood might have matured more slowly than people of his day, but his main solution to the problem was to suggest that they had produced more children than are mentioned in the Bible. If it was accepted that the children named in Genesis were only the important ones, and that they were not necessarily the first-born, then the problem disappeared. The easiest problem to deal with was that of the giants. The tombs of ancient heroes showed them to have been of great stature, and Augustine could even give a recent example. Shortly before the fall of Rome (410 CE), there was a woman in that city who towered above all the people, even though her parents were not as tall as the tallest. In fact, visitors to Rome made a point of trying to catch a glimpse of this woman, so as to marvel at her stature. If this had been true recently, argued Augustine, it was not difficult to accept that in ancient times there had been far more people on earth with such great height.

These explanations offered by Augustine may seem crude to us. But the methods used by him did not differ fundamentally from those used by critical scholars today. In the first place, he was aware of the problems raised by the text because the text appeared to contradict what was known about the world by observation and experience. In dealing with these problems, he:

- compared parts of the text with other parts, as in the demonstration that the years lived before the Flood were of the same length as during and after the flood;
- suggested that the text might omit information, and not, therefore, be a complete record;
- appealed to secular evidence.

By any standards, Augustine was a man of outstanding intellect, and if his work seems to us to be naive, this is only because the resources and expectations of his day were quite different from those of today. In spite of this cultural difference, we can see that parts of the OT were as perplexing to intelligent people fifteen hundred years ago as they were one hundred years ago.

The twelfth century saw the production of one of the greatest books on OT interpretation ever written. Its author was the Jewish philosopher and physician Maimonides (1138–1204), who grew up in a part of Spain under Muslim rule before moving to Egypt, where he wrote *The Guide of the Perplexed* (*c.* 1190).

Muslim civilization had, from the eighth century, enjoyed a renaissance of science and philosophy, in which the philosophy of the fourth-century BCE Greek philosopher Aristotle played an important part. In Muslim Spain, this philosophy was studied with great care, and it had a profound influence upon Maimonides. Whether Aristotle was correctly understood in Muslim Spain is not the issue here. Maimonides became convinced that Aristotle had correctly described the nature and functioning of the visible universe, and that he had rightly taught that God was incorporeal (without body or parts). Maimonides was impatient with religious apologists, including Christians, who began their speculations not with the world as it actually was, but with propositions derived from their imagination, and framed so as to reconcile reality with religious beliefs. 'I shall say to you that the matter is as Themistus puts it', he wrote. 'That which exists does not conform to the various opinions, but rather the correct opinions conform to that which exists' (*Guide*, I, ch. 71).

But could this approach, which accepted the primacy of philosophical and scientific accounts of reality, be reconciled with the Bible? Maimonides believed that it could, and in *The Guide of the Perplexed*, he argued that the prophets, and supremely Moses, were themselves philosophers with a highly developed faculty of imagination. For this reason, the divine law that they taught was the necessary guide for human conduct.

*The Guide* begins with an examination of biblical language, especially with the many 'human' terms used in connection with God: face, hand, image, went up, went down, etc. Whereas these terms might lead us to think that God has a body and parts, this is not the case, and the words cannot be taken at face value. God does not have a face or a hand, and he does not move. He does not even exist in the way that the world and its contents exist. There is also a discussion about prophecy and prophetic inspiration, based upon Aristotelian philosophical teaching about the constitution of man and his intellect. This discussion shows how it is necessary to interpret passages in which God is said to have 'spoken' to his servants. According to Maimonides, no divine communication takes place except through a vision of prophecy or a dream of prophecy. Some passages make this clear: 'The word of the LORD came to Abram in a vision' (Gen. 15.1). Where the vision is not mentioned in a biblical text, it must be assumed. 'It is known and established as a principle that no prophecy and no prophetic revelation come in any way except in a dream or in a vision and through the agency of an angel' (*Guide*, II, ch. 41). A further implication of this is that in 'miraculous' passages such as Genesis 18 where Abraham saw the three men who somehow represented God, Gen. 32.22ff. where Jacob wrestled with an angel, and Num. 22.22ff. where Balaam's she-ass spoke to her master, it was necessary to conclude that these were visions of prophecy, and not happenings that occurred in a normal state.

Some of the views expressed in *The Guide* were not new. Christian tradition had long ceased to take literally statements about God in human terms. Augustine (*City of God*, XI, II) pointed out in regard to Genesis 6.6 that God could not repent, and that the phrase was a metaphor. Long after Maimonides, Calvin would make a similar point about this, and like passages. For Calvin, 'repented' refers to our understanding of God, but not to God as he really is. The greatness of *The Guide* lies in the way in which its author took with the utmost seriousness the world in which he lived, and the way in which that world was understood by science and philosophy. To say this does not, of course, commit us today to the sort of rationalizing solutions that Maimonides seems to have imposed upon the Bible. It shows us, however, that it is no new thing in biblical interpretation to accept that truth is one, that if the Bible has any significance for the world it has significance for the world as it is perceived intelligently, and that a biblical interpretation is not simply a matter of reading the text literally.

Maimonides was faced with the problems mentioned above because, on the whole, he tried to face up to what the text appeared to say at its surface level. In much Christian exegesis up to the Reformation, it was possible to avoid some of these problems because of the belief that the Bible had four levels of meaning: literal, doctrinal, mystical and ethical. In practice, this meant that the OT was allegorized – something found already in the New Testament itself (see Galatians 4.21–30). However, there is no doubt that one of the attractions of the allegorical method was precisely that it enabled interpreters to look for hidden meanings, without having to grapple with the problems raised by the plain meaning of the text. At the Reformation, the allegorical method was largely rejected by the Protestant Churches.

## From the Reformation to 1750

The Reformation in Europe in the first part of the sixteenth century was closely connected with a revival in biblical studies in the fifteenth century. The invention of printing had made Greek and Hebrew Bibles more widely available, and there was a revival of Hebrew studies among Christian scholars. Luther (1483–1546) was a professor of biblical studies, and he devoted the major share of his teaching to the OT. He believed that he was following in the footsteps of St Paul by using a biblical principle in order to determine what in the OT was central, and what was not. The doctrine of justification by faith was based upon the fact that God is for us in Jesus Christ. Where, in the OT, God is seen to be acting for his people, the gospel can be found; and there are anticipations in the OT of the acceptance, by the nations, of the gospel on the basis of faith (e.g. Luther on Psalm 117). Already in Luther there are anticipations of modern critical positions about the authorship of books of the Bible, without any awareness that this could possibly involve unfaithfulness to the Bible. Luther held that while the Pentateuch was Mosaic, it was not necessarily all by Moses. Many of the prophetic books were not necessarily entirely written by the prophets whose name they bore.

Another great leader of the Reformation, Calvin, was a much more systematic commentator than Luther. He was less prepared than Luther to discriminate between what was central in the OT and what was not. But we see that Calvin adopted positions that were more critical than some conservative positions adopted in the nineteenth or twentieth centuries. In dealing with the creation of the waters above the firmament, Calvin allowed that to common sense, it was incredible that there should be waters above the heaven. But it was not incredible if it was allowed that what was described was the creation of the world as it looked to the Israelites. 'He who would learn astronomy, and other recondite arts, let him go elsewhere . . . the waters here meant are such as the rude and unlearned may pereive' (Calvin on Genesis 1.6).

Calvin was using an interesting principle here. These verses did not describe the creation in such a way as to be consistent with any foreseeable scientific discoveries. They were *accommodated* to what unlearned people saw when they looked around them – rain clouds in the sky, and the sun moving round the earth, for example. We may conclude from this that Calvin did not necessarily expect the Bible to provide scientific information about the nature of the universe.

In the aftermath of the Reformation, from the latter part of the sixteenth century and into the seventeenth century, there arose what has been called Protestant scholasticism. In defending themselves against the Roman Catholic Church, and against each other, the Protestant Churches developed rigid doctrinal positions in which the Bible played the subordinate role of supplying proof texts in order to justify Lutheran or Calvinistic or other Protestant positions. Views of biblical inspiration were affirmed that at their most extreme reduced the biblical writers to little more than instruments through which God had dictated his words. As against the early Church, there was little or no interest in textual criticism. It would be unfair to suggest that during this period the Bible was a dead letter. This would be to belittle the great Puritan commentaries, to mention only one example. But it was during this period that there flourished an approach to the Bible of which modern conservatism is the heir. Before the Reformation, while no orthodox Christian doubted that the Bible was inspired, it was also agreed that the rule of faith of the Church was the foundation for its interpretation; and as has been shown, this did not prevent an active critical tradition. In post-Reformation Protestant orthodoxy, while the Bible served to provide proof texts in order to support particular doctrinal positions, it was also believed that this doctrinal position was fully consistent with the Bible, and that ultimately the Bible alone was sufficient. Scripture provided the basis for the interpretation of Scripture; but not in the radical way that we find in Luther. It would not be unfair to say that during this period the critical attitude to the OT was more restricted than it had ever been before in the history of the Church. It was more restricted than in the early Church, and certainly lacked the radicalism of the first flush of the Reformation.

Towards the close of the seventeenth century, the first steps that were to result in the modern critical approach to the OT were taken in an unexpected quarter – the Roman Catholic Church. A French priest, Richard Simon, undertook to expose the errors of Protestants by attacking the foundation of their faith, namely, their belief in the sufficiency of the Bible alone. Two of his lines of attack concern us here. The first concerned the text of the Bible. He argued that in fact we could not be absolutely certain what the original text of the Bible contained, and that Protestants were thus on shaky ground in depending upon the Bible for their faith. They believed in an infallible book whose precise text was uncertain. In support of his arguments, Simon undertook much pioneering research into the history of the text and versions of the Bible. Second, he accused Protestants of confusing authority with authenticity.

Protestants, following traditional Jewish and Christian views about the authorship of books of the Bible, regarded the books as the work of known inspired individuals such as Moses, Joshua, Samuel, David and Solomon. The authority of the Bible was supported by authenticity; that is, the belief that the books had been written by named, inspired individuals. Simon attacked this position by questioning the authenticity, or rather the traditional views of the authorship, of some books. He suggested that much composition had been done by scribal schools, that Moses was not the author of the entire Pentateuch, and that books such as Judges, Samuel and Kings had reached their present form long after the events described. Simon believed that provided Roman Catholic scholars did not contradict the doctrines of the Church, they should be free to investigate such matters as the authorship of the books, and the history of the text of the Bible, in a critical manner. He was too far ahead of his time. His own Church, without ever formally condemning him, frustrated the distribution of his publications. Yet it was not able to prevent his influence, as will be seen later.

Another important movement of the late seventeenth and early eighteenth centuries was Deism, which had its home in England. Deism was a philosophical form of religion that accepted reason as a sufficient guiding principle. It was clear to reason that the world had been created by God, that the soul survived death, and that there were rewards for the righteous and punishments for the wicked. If this was the true, universal form of religion, then particular religions were necessary only for those peoples who were ignorant of reason. In the case of the OT, Deists attacked its apparent lack of belief in an afterlife as well as its low moral standards. Another reason for dissatisfaction with the OT was that the Reformation in England had justified the right of Protestant kings such as Edward VI to reform the national religion by referring to reforming Israelite kings such as Josiah. Deists in eighteenth century England who wished to attack the Established Church could do so by attacking the OT.

Meanwhile, in the eighteenth century, English Deism spread to Germany, where it played a major part in the renewal of German critical scholarship. One of the fathers of the modern critical method in Germany was J.S. Semler. He had been brought up in pietist circles, in a type of Protestantism that laid great stress upon personal experience, especially experience of conversion, and that had been represented in Britain by the Methodist revival of the eighteenth century. In addition to his pietist background, Semler was familiar with English Deist writings, as well as with the work of Richard Simon, which he arranged to have translated into German. Semler was also deeply interested in Luther, whom he studied on the basis of manuscript evidence as well as the semi-reliable printed editions of Luther's works.

Richard Simon had found in the teaching authority of the Church the firm foundation on the basis of which he could conduct his critical investigations of the Bible. Semler found his firm foundation in the doctrine of justification by faith. The primary purpose of Scripture was to speak to the individual the word of assurance by which he knew that God had reconciled him to himself in Jesus Christ. Granted this assurance, the Christian scholar had the liberty to investigate the Bible freely and fearlessly. Semler used the principle of justification as a criterion for defining what was central in the OT. Where the OT described the work of God in vindicating his people, there was the gospel. Other material was less important. With the work of Semler, the era of the modern historical critical study of the OT can be said to have begun.

## *The new element in critical study from 1750*

Was critical study of the OT fundamentally different after roughly 1750 from what it was previously? If so, what has been the point in this essay of trying to show that, in one sense, OT study has always been critical? With regard to the methods of critical scholarship after 1750 compared with before that date, there was no fundamental difference. In both periods, scholars were concerned with textual criticism and with the study of the biblical languages. In both, what was known about the history, customs and physical geography of the land of the Bible was collected and studied. In both, scholars tried to face up to the problems raised by apparent contradictions between the Bible and philosophical and scientific accounts of the world. What was new after 1750 was that critical investigation was prepared to be critical of the doctrinal positions of churches. Before 1750, even the most radical investigations in mainstream Christianity or Judaism were bound ultimately to stay within certain bounds. Maimonides accepted, and devoutly believed in, the superiority of Moses and the divine origin of the Mosaic law. Simon was a devout Roman Catholic who did not doubt the teaching authority of his Church. It would be wrong to suggest that after 1750 scholars ceased to be devout, and that the openness of their method inevitably led to scepticism and heresy, although this was the charge commonly brought against critical scholars in the nineteenth century. If a critical scholar believed, with Semler, that the Bible spoke words of assurance of reconciliation to God through Jesus Christ, it is difficult to see how this could lead to scepticism, unless Christianity was defined in such a way as to commit all believers to particular views about who had written the books of the Bible. And it was not only in the circles of critical scholarship that 'heresy' could arise. Orthodox Protestantism in the seventeenth and eighteenth centuries produced 'Unitarianism' among those who so upheld the sufficiency of the Bible that they rejected any sort of assent to the doctrine of the Trinity as defined in the early Church and reaffirmed at the Reformation, because the Bible itself did not require such assent from believers.

On the other hand, once it was conceded that the Bible could challenge church doctrines, it was possible for scholars to reach conclusions at variance with Christianity. Of course, long before 1750, the study of the Bible had led some people to views that were against the prevailing orthodoxy, with the result that they left, or were excluded from, their churches. After 1750, it was easier in some churches for those with unorthodox views to remain in membership. The difference between the situation before 1750 and that after can, perhaps, be summed up as follows. Before 1750, critical scholarship was ultimately a defence of whatever type of orthodoxy a scholar accepted, for all that far-reaching concessions might well be made to contemporary philosophic or scientific views. After 1750, critical scholars were more prepared to let their biblical scholarship challenge their own orthodoxy. Their scholarship was far more an open-ended quest for truth than a quest for truth limited by acceptance of an orthodoxy, whether that orthodoxy was concerned with the verbal inspiration of Scripture, or the teaching authority of the Roman Catholic Church.

It is at this point that it may be correct to identify the difficulty that new students experience. The use made of the Bible in churches is very properly a use directed towards specific evangelistic, doctrinal and theological ends. Preachers worth their salt do not spend time in the pulpit pointing out difficulties the Bible contains. They make a positive proclamation. On the other hand, ordinary worshippers are aware that the Bible is not a simple book to understand, and that it appears to be in conflict with modern scientific accounts of the world. In some cases, churches may help worshippers tackle these critical questions through study groups. In other cases, there may be no occasion when worshippers can discuss their difficulties openly, and they may either conclude for themselves, or be told straight out, that it is un-Christian to entertain the idea that critical questions can be addressed to the Bible. But one of the points of the first part of this historical sketch of biblical criticism has been to show that it is quite false to equate a questioning and critical attitude with unfaithfulness to the Bible. It cannot be maintained that it is wrong to ask critical questions, and wrong to use reason and the intellect to try to solve critical problems. If we accept this, then we condemn Augustine, Luther, Calvin and many others. Nevertheless, it appears to be true that, because many beginners in biblical studies do not have, nor can be expected to have, any knowledge of the history of critical study, they are upset or put off even by the sort of critical approaches that existed before 1750, in the so-called pre-critical period.

At the end of this essay, some of the points made in this section will be mentioned again. It now remains to sketch the development of the critical method from 1750.

## From 1750

In the first half of the eighteenth century, England had been far ahead of Germany in the critical investigation of the OT. From 1750 the positions were reversed. Deism declined in England, and the rapid spread of pietistic forms of Christianity led to the emergence of the Methodist connexions and also affected parts of the Church of England. A period of religious conservatism began that lasted until at least the 1860s, and that confined critical biblical study to the Unitarians and a small group of liberal Anglicans. Resistance in England to biblical criticism was strengthened from the late 1820s by the Oxford Movement's reaffirmation of the Catholic roots of the Church of England.

In Germany, where there were more than twenty Protestant theological faculties in universities at a time when England had only two universities (and Scotland five!), there began to emerge a body of critical scholarship sustained by the production of scholarly journals and supported by a university career structure that required aspiring scholars to undertake original research in order to obtain the doctorates and licences necessary for their advancement. Mention has been made of J.S. Semler; other notable German scholars of the latter half of the eighteenth century were J.G. Eichhorn, who published the first introduction to the Old Testament (*Einleitung in das Alte Testament*, 1780), and J.D. Michaelis, who published extensively on the laws, customs and geography of the ancient Israelites. Important contributions were also made by J.G. Herder, a leading literary and philosophical figure (he was primarily employed as a Lutheran clergyman) who researched into the opening chapters of Genesis and was a pioneer in the writing of universal history, including the history of Israel.

By the beginning of the nineteenth century, many positions that would later become commonplace in biblical criticism had been suggested in Germany. However, a crucial breakthrough came in 1806–7, when W.M.L. de Wette suggested that the actual history of Israelite religion had been quite different from what is presented in the OT itself. According to the OT, Israel's system of priesthood, law and sacrifice was revealed to Moses by God during the wilderness wanderings. De Wette argued that this system had developed slowly over many generations, and that because figures such as Samuel and Elijah knew nothing about the command in Deuteronomy that sacrifice should be offered only at a single sanctuary (Elijah in 1 Kings 19.10 complains that the Israelites have destroyed the altars, something that is *commanded* in Deuteronomy 12.3!), this proved that Deuteronomy could not have been written until the seventh century.

It is important to consider what was new in de Wette's position. Prior to him, no one had radically questioned the overall historical picture of ancient Israel's history as presented in the OT. Radical scholars may have attacked church doctrines and Deists may have poured scorn on certain aspects of OT morality, but it had been accepted that the general historical outline was accurate. De Wette changed this by using research into how and when the OT was written to produce a reconstructed history of Israel's religion that was at variance with what the OT said. This was a radical turn in critical scholarship that has affected the discipline ever since. In this book, its implications will be discussed in the chapter on OT history.

For the remainder of the nineteenth century, OT scholarship struggled to come to terms with de Wette's radical turn. Initially accepted by several younger scholars, de Wette's views were rejected from around 1835, partly because of an upsurge of confessional orthodoxy in some of the Lutheran churches and partly because of the work of scholars such as Heinrich Ewald, who was a thoroughly critical scholar, but who accepted the general outline of Israel's history as presented in the OT. It was not until the 1860s that scholars began to do de Wette's basic work all over again, and there began to emerge a view of Israel's history that was indebted to his pioneering research. The name most usually connected with this view is that of Julius Wellhausen; but whereas Wellhausen's *Geschichte Israels* (History of Israel) of 1878 was a classic exposition of the new position (better known in his 1883 *Prolegomena to the History of Israel*), Wellhausen was only one of the main researchers, and in any case, he readily acknowledged his debt to de Wette. Other important contributors were the Dutch scholar Abraham Kuenen and the Scot William Robertson Smith, whose *Old Testament in the Jewish Church* (1881) remains the most brilliant and original exposition of the new position, and all the more remarkable because Smith was a committed evangelical who believed in the necessity of biblical criticism for advancing the evangelical cause.

Basically, the new position divided Israel's religion into three periods. The first, up to the seventh century, was a period of many sanctuaries, each with a local priesthood, and one in which

Israelites worshipped with Canaanites and adopted some of their customs. In this period were composed the documents J and E (so called because they used the divine names Jahweh and Elohim for God) that are found in Genesis, Exodus and Numbers. Towards the end of this time, prophets such as Hosea, Amos, Isaiah and Micah sharply criticized the morality of the rulers and people as well as their lax attitude to religion. This led to the second period, that of Josiah's reform in the seventh century (622 BCE) based upon Deuteronomy (D according to the Documentary Hypothesis). Local sanctuaries were closed down, and Jerusalem was declared to be the only legitimate place of sacrifice (although Jerusalem is not actually mentioned in Deuteronomy). The third period, from the exile, was the one in which the sacrificial and priestly legislation contained in Exodus, Leviticus and Numbers was composed and recorded in the Priestly Document (P), to serve the needs of the post-exilic community.

Although one of the contributors to this new view was British (Robertson Smith), its acceptance in Britain was far from easy. Smith himself was tried for heresy and in 1881 dismissed by the Free Church of Scotland from his post at the Free Church College in Aberdeen. Such critical scholarship as had begun to emerge in Britain in the 1860s inclined towards the more traditional position maintained by Ewald. Also, from 1828 to 1882 E.B. Pusey, the Regius Professor of Hebrew at Oxford and a leading member of the Oxford Movement, resolutely opposed any encroachment of critical scholarship into England, believing it to be ultimately a threat to Christian belief in the divinity of Jesus. A change came in 1883 with the succession to the Oxford Hebrew chair of S.R. Driver. At first very cautious about accepting the new view, he was gradually convinced by it, and in his *Introduction to the Literature of the Old Testament* (1891) provided what is still the best introduction in English to the so-called Documentary Hypothesis and its implications for the history of Israel's religion. Driver was also concerned to reconcile intelligent use of the Bible with scientific belief, especially the theory of evolution, and his commentary on Genesis (1904) was said to have saved the faith of a generation.

In the United States of America biblical criticism was strongly stimulated by contact with Germany. The Boston Unitarian Theodore Parker translated some of de Wette's work, while Edward Robinson studied under the great Halle lexicographer

Wilhelm Gesenius, undertook pioneering research in Palestine, and prepared a translation of Gesenius's Hebrew Dictionary that later became the basis for the famous Hebrew Lexicon of Brown, Driver and Briggs.

However, the introduction of the critical method in the United States did not escape opposition. The second half of the nineteenth century saw the rise of dispensational pre-millenarianism, which developed the old idea that God was dealing with mankind through successive covenants, or dispensations. Dispensationalism was a sophisticated method of biblical interpretation that partitioned biblical history into distinct phases. Some of these phases were relevant only to God's plans for the Jews, and they had no direct application to the Church apart from being evidence for divine activity. Dispensationalism totally rejected all forms of historical or literary criticism as applied to the Bible. Towards the end of the nineteenth century, controversy within the Presbyterian Church of America about the inspiration of the Bible led to the trials for heresy of two prominent OT scholars, Charles A. Briggs of Union Seminary, New York (1893), and Henry Preserved Smith of Lane Seminary, Cincinnati (1894). Both were later contributors to the outstanding Anglo-American *International Critical Commentary*. Briggs had studied in Berlin with Emil Rödiger, and had a deep knowledge of German critical scholarship.

## *Modern conservatism and biblical criticism*

The academic and critical study of the Bible in Britain is largely undertaken in departments in secular universities. (The situation in the United States is, of course, rather more complex.) In many cases, universities have statutes prohibiting denominational religious teaching. In such university departments, the teaching is based upon research, which is itself based upon the fundamental tenet of the critical method, namely, that scholars are free to follow in their work what they sincerely believe to be the truth, even if that questions religious and academic assumptions that they hold. The content of the syllabuses is to some degree determined by what happen to be the central issues in scholarship at the time (see the opening of this chapter). Universities are not the only places where the Bible is studied. There are theological colleges or seminaries, and Bible and missionary training colleges. In these, the OT may well be studied critically, but usually within the limits of the specific aims of these colleges. It is no part of this essay to suggest that what these institutions do is wrong, or unacademic. Students who come to study the Bible at university enter an academic discipline as rigorous as any. They are required to be something of a linguist, a historian, and a person with literary and artistic appreciation. Students who come from conservative backgrounds may suffer from an initial shock. They may come from a type of Christianity that is descended from the later phase of the Reformation in the late sixteenth and seventeenth centuries. As has been seen above, this phase was a good deal less critical than the scholarship that was found in the early Church and the beginning of the Reformation.

Whatever beliefs students may bring with them when they begin their academic studies, it is not right for university departments to try to destroy those beliefs, and to substitute for them the opinions of the teachers. This would amount to an infringement of the intellectual integrity of a student. Students must rather be presented with the evidence, the resources for tackling questions, and some guidance about elementary logic, so that they may reach their own conclusions.

There is one question that the present writer has often put to his more conservative students, and that can serve to end this chapter. The Bible says of itself that it is inspired by God (2 Timothy 3.16). Does this statement necessarily mean that only traditional views of the authorship of books of the Bible can be correct? Does it necessarily exclude the possibility that books had more than one writer, and that literary sources were used? On what grounds is it permissible to limit the power of God by saying that although he could have inspired one writer of a biblical book, he could not possibly have inspired several authors or redactors? Critical views of the origin and growth of the Bible do not, as is often suggested, undermine belief in the inspiration and authority of the Bible, even if they may demand different ways of using the Bible as compared with 'literal' or 'dispensational' ways of reading it. Critical views, by showing the complexity and indeed the 'ordinariness' of the growth of the Bible, require a deep and sophisticated view of the divine guiding as a result of which the Bible is *not* like any other book, even when it is studied critically like any other book.

## NOTES

For a specialist treatment of the origins of biblical criticism in the United States see J.W. Brown, *The Rise of Biblical Criticism in America, 1400–1870* (Middletown, Wesleyan University, 1969). For a Roman Catholic view see Jean Levie, *The Bible, Word of God in Words of Men* (London, Geoffrey Chapman, 1961; New York, P.J. Kennedy, 1962). For a detailed discussion of Fundamentalism see J. Barr, *Fundamentalism* (London, SCM, 1977; Philadelphia, Westminster, 1978).

## FURTHER READING

R.E. Clements, *A Century of Old Testament Study* (Guildford, Lutterworth, 1976, revised ed. 1983).

— *One Hundred Years of Old Testament Interpretation* (Philadelphia, Westminster, 1976).

J. Drury (ed.), *Critics of the Bible 1724–1873* (Cambridge, Cambridge University Press, 1989).

J.W. Rogerson, 'Interpretation, History of', in *The Anchor Bible Dictionary* (New York, Doubleday, 1992), vol. 3 pp. 425–33.

— 'The Old Testament', in J. Rogerson, C. Rowland, B. Lindars, *The Study and Use of the Bible* (Basingstoke, Marshall Pickering; Grand Rapids, Eerdmans, 1988), pp. 1–150.

— *Old Testament Criticism in the Nineteenth Century – England and Germany* (London, SPCK, 1984).

K. Scholder, *The Birth of Modern Critical Theology – Origins and Problems of Biblical Criticism in the Seventeenth Century* (London, SCM; Philadelphia, Trinity Press International, 1990).

# 2

# Methods in Old Testament Study

## DAVID J. A. CLINES

Methods are a means to an end; so before we speak of methods in academic Old Testament study, we must speak of *goals* in OT study. Many, perhaps most, people come to the study of the Bible with religious goals in mind: they want to know more about the Bible because they believe it will deepen their faith, communicate God's will to them, and so on. They have a preconception about the nature of the Bible. Perhaps it is for them the word of God, the final authority in matters of faith and practice; or perhaps they see it rather as the deposit of the religious experiences of ancient Jews and Christians, a valuable resource book for religious believers of today. Nevertheless, those who have religious goals as their aim need to realize that biblical study of itself will not achieve those goals, though it would be surprising if it did not have a great deal of religious pay-off (to put it crudely). The academic study of the Bible has been, and must be, one in which people of any religious faith, or of none, can engage and can co-operate. The immediate goal of academic biblical study must be one that allows but does not require religious preconceptions; for many, the immediate goal may be only a stage on the way to an ultimate (religious) goal, but for others it may be a sufficient goal in itself.

In the first edition of this book, I suggested that the primary goal in biblical study should be *understanding*. Other goals people have in studying the OT, like learning Hebrew or discovering the facts about the history of Israel or passing examinations, even life goals like deepening one's religious faith or becoming a wiser person, can best be regarded as secondary goals in the *academic* study of the OT. For only some goal like 'understanding the texts' can be in tune with the nature of academic study.

Given that there is an Old Testament (or as we should perhaps call it, Hebrew Bible), what else can be done with it in an institution of higher education? It cannot be preached, and it cannot be 'taught' – as doctrine, that is, as what one ought to believe; for a university or college is not the place for that. But neither can it be used simply as a textbook for ancient history or as a source for illustrating social customs in the ancient Near East; for it was self-evidently not for these purposes that the Hebrew Bible was brought together in the form that it has, and it does not as a whole have the character of a history or a manual of social customs. Only some description like 'the Scriptures of the Hebrew people', or 'the sacred writings of the Jews which now also form part of the Christian Bible', can do justice to its essence. It is a strange combination of history and religion and literature, and the most appropriate way of handling such a document in an academic setting would seem to be to attempt to *understand* it.

Now that I come to prepare a revision of this chapter for the second edition of the book, I have to say that I am not so sure that understanding should necessarily be the primary goal in biblical study. One might well go on to ask what the purpose of such understanding is, what one is going to do with one's understanding, what difference it may make to you if you understand it, and how understanding it may change you. Once we ask questions of this kind, we imply that there are goals beyond understanding. A Marxist formulation has it is that the point is not to understand the world but to change it – which means to say that if you already regard the world as unjust, oppressive and the like, merely going on understanding how unjust it is would be rather a waste of time; what an unjust world needs is to be changed into something better. Or if we think of ills and evils like cancer or poverty, we might also agree that to rest content with understanding them, their causes and their nature would be a rather inhuman thing to do; what we really want is to prevent them or alleviate them. And if we think of goods and benefits like happiness or job satisfaction, who would be satisfied with merely understanding them and how they come about, when it might be possible to enhance people's lives by creating more of them?

So, when it comes to the OT, what goals in the study of it could there be beyond understanding? My answer is: *evaluation* or *critique* (on the basis of understanding, of course). I would not want the academic study of the Bible to be an opportunity for people to express their prejudices either for or against the Bible, but I would like to see biblical scholars throw off some of their traditional reserve and their stance of 'objectivity' and frankly say what it is about the Bible they want to affirm (if anything) and what it is they cannot adhere to (if anything) – that is, to express their own personal evaluation of the material they are doing their best to understand. Otherwise, I do not see that we are being honest with ourselves and fair to our students.

It happens that the last fifteen years, the period since the first edition of this book was published, have seen an upsurge of biblical study of kinds that can be called critique or evaluation. I am referring to the methods in criticism that go under the heading of 'post-structuralism', of which feminist, ideological and materialist criticisms are perhaps the most notable. I shall be dealing with them in the second section of this chapter, as 'second-order methods' of OT study. All that needs to be said here is that none of them can dispense with understanding. Though understanding the OT may not be the only worthwhile thing to do with it, there is nothing academic we can do with it at all if we do not make the utmost attempt to understand it, the parts and the whole, in its own terms and for its own sake.

There are other academic goals we can have in the study of the OT that are neither understanding nor evaluation, properly speaking. These are goals we might have when our intention is to *use* the OT for some other academic purpose, such as, for example, reconstructing the history of ancient Israel, establishing what daily life in ancient Israel was like, or learning the classical Hebrew language. These are all proper academic goals, and all of them will have something to contribute to our understanding of the Hebrew Bible. But they are not in themselves attempts at understanding or evaluation of the OT, and so I will be referring to them in the third section of this chapter as 'third-order methods' of OT study. They too require understanding of the Hebrew Bible itself, and so modes of understanding will be the 'first-order methods' of biblical study and the first section of this chapter.

## *First-order methods*

Since we are speaking of understanding as the first of our goals in OT study, let us be clear about the terms we should use. When we come to formulate any understanding we gain, whether of part or of the whole of the OT, we call that formulation or putting into words an interpretation. Now, since it is probably impossible to understand anything without putting it into words, at least in one's own mind, one might as well say perhaps that interpretation should be the chief aim of OT study. I prefer, however, to say 'understanding', since that focuses on the processes by which one comes to understand, rather than 'interpretation', which focuses on the crystallization of that understanding. Nevertheless, using the term interpretation is a useful reminder of what kind of writing about the OT is most appropriate to its nature. Those works that illuminate the text by offering an interpretation, whether of a phrase or a book, the meaning of a verse or the structure of a biblical author's thought, are the most suited to its character. While not all commentaries are illuminating, the commentary form is the quintessential mode of biblical interpretation; but the essay on character, plot or theology can be equally valuable for the interpretation of larger passages.

One other term, frequently encountered in biblical studies, needs to be introduced at this point, namely exegesis. Exegesis is in fact nothing but interpretation, but the term is usually reserved for the kind of interpretation that explains phrase by phrase or verse by verse the biblical passage; interpretation may refer to a more discursive treatment of longer stretches of biblical text.

Biblical interpretation has been going on for a long time (see Chapter 1), ever since any part of the Bible was composed, in fact, for every hearer or reader is an interpreter of what he or she hears or reads – otherwise we do not understand what we hear or read. Certain methods that have been successful in biblical interpretation have acquired names familiar to biblical scholars – though they may be unfamiliar to many experts in the interpretation of other literary texts. I will first discuss three of these methods traditional in biblical scholarship, and then three other methods more familiar to students of other literatures. None of the methods discussed in this chapter is wholly distinct from other methods; some have fairly clear procedures, while others are more an approach or an attitude to the text; there is no predetermined sequence in which these methods can most fruitfully be applied, and no way of telling in advance which will yield the best results; and in many cases a method is not very different from common sense, so that one is not always aware of using a particular method.

## TRADITIONAL METHODS IN BIBLICAL SCHOLARSHIP

*Historical–grammatical exegesis* This is in fact not so much a method, but more a way of life to most biblical scholars. The term refers to the endeavour to interpret any passage according to the natural sense of the words ('grammatical') and according to the probable meaning of the author in his or her own time ('historical'). As a method, it functions first as a warning against arbitrary or fanciful interpretations, such as were often (but not invariably) to be encountered in pre-Reformation interpretation. Thus, while an allegorical interpretation of the OT often saw in the name Jerusalem a veiled reference to the pious Christian soul or to the heavenly city, the historical–*grammatical* method insists that 'Jerusalem' in the OT always refers to the ancient city of that name, unless there is good evidence to the contrary. Or, whereas the commentary on the prophecy of Habakkuk composed by members of the Dead Sea scrolls community at Qumran apparently interpreted the 'righteous' and 'wicked' referred to by Habakkuk (in the late seventh century BCE) as persons contemporary with the Qumran community, in the first century BCE, the *historical*–grammatical method insists that these words should refer to those persons intended by the prophet. (In this case, it is clear that Hab. 1.4 refers to 'righteous' and 'wicked' men of Habakkuk's own time.)

Such an approach may seem obvious enough to us, but we may note that it may lead to apparent loss of understanding rather than gain. Thus the statement of God in Gen. 1.26, 'Let us make humanity in our image', was readily interpreted by early Christian scholars as an address by God the Father to the other persons of the Trinity, since God is speaking of 'us' in the plural. As exegetes of the historical–grammatical school, we ourselves would deny that the author of Genesis 1 knew anything of the doctrine of the Trinity, since Genesis was written well before the advent of Christianity and the formulation of the doctrine of the Trinity; so we would deny that such can be the meaning. Nonetheless, we seem to be no better off than the early Christian scholars, for though many suggestions have been made, no entirely convincing interpretation of the plural can be offered. In such cases, we can only plead that to understand less is not necessarily to understand worse. Again, the historical–grammatical method can *create* problems that do not exist if its rigours are not applied. So references in the Psalms to the king, especially to the king as God's son (Ps. 2.7), were traditionally interpreted by Christian scholars as references to the Messiah, Christ. If the historical–grammatical method is followed, however, the king must be seen as the contemporary Israelite king, and some explanation must be found for references to him as God's son and for the address to him as 'God' (Ps. 45.6 – if that is what the Hebrew actually says).

Despite such problems, the historical–grammatical approach is universally accepted, principally because it offers a criterion for judging between rival interpretations. It is not so clear to all scholars today, however, as it was even a few decades ago, that the meaning of a passage should be restricted to 'the meaning intended by the author'. This doubt arises partly because authors (especially poets) do not always intend one meaning and one meaning only, and partly because re-applications of a prophet's words (for example) to later situations – a process that was going on already in the OT period and that is clearly evident in the New Testament – can be argued to draw out fresh, legitimate, meanings from those words that the prophet himself never intended. Even more important, it is also commonly argued today that the meaning of words is whatever they mean to readers, and that authors have no control over what their words are taken to mean. This is a truly radical issue; but it is doubtful whether the historical–grammatical approach can ever be dispensed with, and the meaning we presume the author intended will always be an important constituent, though not the sum total, of our interpretation of a passage.

*Textual criticism*    Historical–grammatical exegesis interprets the texts; but what is the text? We do not have the original manuscripts of any biblical book. The oldest Hebrew manuscripts come from the second century BCE, but they are mostly fragmentary; the oldest datable complete Hebrew Bible is from the eleventh century CE. While all the evidence shows that on the whole the original texts of the biblical writings have been copied faithfully down through the centuries, in the exact wording there are thousands of variations. It is impossible to know with complete precision what the books of Amos or Job, for example, originally said; but it is possible to reconstruct a 'better' text than exists in any surviving manuscript – that is, a text more likely to be near the original text.

The discipline that strives to reach behind the medieval

manuscripts to the probable precise wording of the biblical books is known as textual criticism. In many respects it is a rigorously objective discipline, with elaborate rules for the evaluation of any piece of textual evidence. From another point of view, however, it is a form of interpretation, since the ultimate arbiter of any textual evidence is the scholar's (or scholars') judgement about its intelligibility. So the fact that all the manuscripts and the ancient versions (in some cases centuries older than our Hebrew manuscripts) agree on the wording of a verse does not necessarily mean that the verse makes sense or that it reproduces what the author originally wrote. In Amos 6.12, for example, the Hebrew and the versions have 'Does one plough with oxen?' in a sequence of rhetorical questions that are meant to be answered 'No!' There seems to be some mistake in the Hebrew, since this particular question is one that we would answer with 'Yes!' An emendation (i.e. proposed correction) of the Hebrew yields the sense 'Does one plough the sea with oxen?' ('No!') – which is just the absurd kind of question required by the context; RSV, NEB and most modern versions translate accordingly, convinced that this is more probably what Amos said. (What is involved is dividing one Hebrew word into two and supplying different vowels, *bbqr ym*, pronounced *babbāqār yām*, instead of *bbqrym*, pronounced *babbeqār î m*.) Another situation arises when the ancient versions agree in differing from the Hebrew text. A well-known example occurs in Gen. 4.8, where the Hebrew manuscripts have 'Cain said to Abel his brother' but do not tell us what he said (the Hebrew verb does mean 'said' rather than 'spoke'). Several of the ancient versions of the Bible, namely the Samaritan text of the Pentateuch, the Greek Septuagint, the Latin Vulgate, and two of the three Aramaic Targums (paraphrasing translations), have Cain say to Abel something like 'Let us go into the fields' (where Cain is intending to kill Abel). Here the only rule a textual critic can offer by way of advice is not very helpful: he or she will say, judiciously, that the Samaritan and the Greek when agreeing against the Hebrew of Genesis are not necessarily preferable. So in the end scholars must decide whether they think the ancient versions have preserved a phrase accidentally omitted from the Hebrew, or whether the ancient versions have made an addition to the Hebrew because they were as puzzled by the Hebrew as we are. Among modern translations, the RSV and NIV insert the addition, explaining in a footnote that the addition is based on the ancient versions, while the NEB inserts it without explaining that it is an addition; the RV fudged the issue by translating 'Cain *told* Abel his brother' (though the Hebrew cannot mean 'told' rather than 'said'!).

It is often thought that textual criticism provides a foundation upon which exegesis builds; the examples above show that while most of the business of textual criticism (collecting evidence, generalizing about the tendencies of a version or the relationship of manuscripts) is not exegesis and could be regarded as preparatory to it, the point of decision in a matter of textual criticism belongs to the work of interpretation. Establishing the text and interpreting the text are enterprises that go hand in hand.

*Redaction criticism*   A 'redactor' is the jargon in biblical studies for what is usually called in other literary studies an 'editor'. The term comes from the stage in biblical criticism when the authors of biblical books (e.g. the Gospels) were regarded as essentially compilers or editors of sources rather than as authors in their own right. But today, when authors of biblical books are increasingly seen as more than merely editors, the rather misleading term 'redaction criticism' is still applied to the search for the distinctive viewpoint, or intention, of the author that is expressed in the shape and organization of his work, its contents, its principle of selection and omission, as well as in express statements of intention by the author. English-speaking scholars have not adopted the German word sometimes used for such study, *Tendenz* or 'tendency' criticism, though this is a more appropriate term.

An example of where 'redaction' or 'tendency' criticism can be applied to good effect is the history work running from Joshua to 2 Kings, known as the 'Deuteronomistic History' because the style and outlook of the author have much in common with the book of Deuteronomy. A careful reader of this history will not imagine that it was written simply to record the past, but will find in it clues to the author's intention, purpose, or bias. Some of the evidence is explicit, as in his famous judgements upon the kings of Israel and Judah that they 'did evil [or occasionally, 'good'] in the eyes of the LORD'. Some of the evidence is implicit, as in the fact that he included many narratives of prophetic figures (e.g. Elijah and Elisha) and that he began his work with Joshua and the Judges and ended it with the fall of

Jerusalem. Putting all the evidence together, we may say that the author's purpose was to establish that the monarchy was an institution fatal for Israel, or that the destruction of Israel and Judah came about because they gave too little heed to the prophets or because the worship of foreign gods was tolerated in Israel – or some more subtle blending of such statements. However we define the intention or 'tendency' of the work, by doing so we are fashioning a major interpretative tool for the understanding of the whole work and each of its parts.

Redaction criticism in the strictest sense is a study of how the author used his sources. In the case of the Deuteronomistic History, the sources are mostly hypothetical, though it is entirely reasonable to suppose that some parts were drawn from royal annals, some from a collection of stories, whether written or oral, about heroes ('judges'), some from a series of tales about prophets. If the sources can be reconstructed with any degree of certainty and if the author's own shaping of them (addition, deletion, compression, etc.) can be detected, we have further evidence to put toward our comprehensive picture of his 'tendency'. In the study of the Gospels, if we can be sure that Matthew used Mark as a written source, redaction criticism can be very finely tuned to take into account minute deviations by the author from his source. But more often than not, the same results can be obtained by focusing upon the work itself and upon the interrelationship of its parts.

Redaction criticism, however it is understood, is an aspect of the historical–grammatical approach, and not really another method to be ranked alongside it. Its concern, however, is more with the meaning of the writing as a whole than with the small parts that exegesis is devoted to. And its prominence in recent decades is symptomatic of current interest in larger wholes rather than verse-by-verse details – but both the wholes and the parts have to be studied in careful balance.

## METHODS IN LITERARY CRITICISM

*Rhetorical criticism*   Rhetorical criticism concerns itself with the way the language of texts is deployed to convey meaning. Its interests are in the devices of writing, in metaphor and parallelism, in narrative and poetic structures, in stylistic figures. In principle, it is also interested in the original situation of the composition and promulgation of ancient texts, and in their intended effect upon their audience. But its primary focus is upon the texts and the way they hang together and the way they work, rather than upon their historical setting. In English literature studies, what biblical critics call 'rhetorical criticism' is often known as 'close reading', a minute attention to the words and images of the text.

Poetry is often a more immediately rewarding subject for rhetorical criticism or close reading than is prose. A biblical example that lends itself well to close reading is Hosea's fine poem about Yahweh and his adulterous wife Israel (Hos. 2.2–23). If we concentrate upon the primary image of the poem, that of the relationship, we sense the dominance of indicators of *belonging*: *my* wife, *her* husband, *her* children, *their* mother, *my* lovers, *my* wool, *my* flax, *my* oil, *my* drink, and many other such phrases. If we see that this is a poem about belonging, we have not tamed it or pigeonholed it, but we have sharpened our perception of it. We can go on to consider what kinds of belonging exist in the poem: there is *right* belonging ('my husband', v. 16) and *negation* of belonging ('not my wife', v.2) and wrong belonging ('my lovers', v.5). The whole poem, it turns out, explores this triple possibility in belonging. The acts of movement (coming, going, returning), of gift (giving, withholding, taking), of thought (remembering, forgetting, remembering wrongly), and of speech (responding, not responding, responding wrongly) are all developments of the fundamental three-way division in the primary image. The more these connections and resemblances are dwelt on and savoured, the more the poem manifests its unity of conception, and the deeper, consequently, the reader's understanding of it.

The rhetorical criticism of a passage (a poem perhaps, or a whole book), while it requires wholehearted concentration upon that text, does not demand that all other texts should be expunged from one's mind (if that were possible!), though some critics of 'close reading' have supposed that it does. For obviously one's general knowledge of life and particular knowledge of other works of the same author, or in the case of the OT, other OT books, contribute – often unconsciously – to one's understanding of a passage; the commentaries draw explicit attention to all kinds of such extraneous data. There is another type of extraneous knowledge, however, that can be very valuable, even though it may be knowledge of what may not exist (!). That is to say, every text has a countertext, or rather, many countertexts – things that could have been said, but weren't. What is actually spoken or written is always selected, consciously or not, from the countless possibilities inherent in the language known to the speaker or writer. Every sentence spoken or written has un-expressed and rejected counterparts lurking in the background. By conjuring up some of these countertexts, the reality, in-dividuality and lack of inevitability of the text before us can be reinforced. We call up such a countertext when we read in Isa. 53.2 that the servant of Yahweh 'grew up before him like a young plant, like a plant rooted in dry ground', and remark that the last phrase is hardly what we would expect; for the righteous in the OT are generally not weedy and underdeveloped, and if they are like plants, they are like plants by streams of water whose leaf does not wither (Ps. 1.3). To the servant of Yahweh is attributed a history contrary to expectation (hence the astonishment of onlookers, 52.14), and the countertext, which in this case exists in the background and which we are at least vaguely aware of, focuses our attention on something peculiar and unique about Isaiah 53 and so enriches our understanding.

*The idea of the 'literary work of art'*   Whatever else the OT is, it is beyond question a literary work. There are some parts of it, indeed, that could hardly be called 'literature' (e.g. the genealogies at the beginning of 1 Chronicles), except perhaps on a minimalist definition of literature as merely 'something written'. But the great majority is literature – chiefly of the types story and poem – of varying degrees of quality. Therefore the best-suited approaches in studying it are, not surprisingly, those that are effective in literature studies more generally. One such approach is the stress in literature studies of the last half-century especially on the idea of the 'literary work of art'. This phrase stands for two distinct emphases:

1  that the literary work should be primarily considered as a whole
2  that the literary work should be studied for what it is in itself, with relatively minor concentration on the historical circumstances of its composition.

(1) The first emphasis is one that has emerged in biblical studies in the development of redaction criticism (see above). In literary criticism, it balances the stress on close reading, which without the constraint of the total view can easily lead to atomistic interpretation. The holistic, total view, while always open to

revision in the light of the merest detail, must have the last word in interpretation. In the quest for the historical–grammatical meaning, the essence, message, function, purpose (some terms are at times more appropriate than others) of the work as a whole is our ultimate ambition. We shall ask how the parts fit together, how the parts succeed in producing the whole, and whether the whole is supported by the parts. But at the end of the day it is the *whole* (whether a psalm or the book of Job or the Pentateuch), in the articulation of its parts, and in its manifold variety, that should be the object of our quest.

This principle has been frequently neglected or positively negated in much biblical criticism. It is still hailed as something of a *tour de force*, for example, if a scholar offers an interpretation of the book of Job that takes into account all its parts. So many chapters of the book (the poem on wisdom, ch.28; the Elihu speeches, chs 32–37; the first or second divine speeches, chs 38–41; the epilogue, 42.7–17) have been regarded by one scholar or another as secondary (i.e. not part of the original book), that the majority of interpretations of the book ignore the doubtful chapters or, indeed, interpret them in a sense at variance with the remainder of the book. The principle of the 'literary work of art', however, operates upon the fact that the book of Job, in all its 42 chapters, is the book that exists, and must therefore be the primary object of our interpretative scrutiny. If some parts seem hard to reconcile with other parts, we need not jump to the conclusion that the book is fundamentally at cross purposes with itself (though that is a possible conclusion, to be reached only at the end of a long and tiring road), but must seek to understand what a book so seemingly at variance with itself could possibly signify when taken as a whole.

If the thrust of the 'literary work of art' is toward 'whole' meanings rather than meanings of the parts, the dangers of the verse-by-verse interpretation, such as is followed in many commentaries and much classroom teaching, become all too clear. Unless one moves constantly between the part and the whole, the particular and the general, what appears to be a worthily thorough and detailed interpretation may in fact be a steadfast and systematic refusal to confront the primary questions of meaning.

(2) The second emphasis of the 'literary work of art' approach, that the work should be studied primarily for what it is in itself, is common ground for a majority of critics of English literature, for

example, but fairly revolutionary in biblical studies. More commonly, OT scholars have insisted that an OT writing can only be interpreted in the light of history, and have gone on from there to demand the most minute historical reconstruction as a prerequisite of interpretation. Some literary critics have gone to the opposite extreme, and argued for the complete 'autonomy' of the literary work of art, which is to say that external information about the authors, their historical and social setting, their sources and the influences upon them are all irrelevant to meaning. But a moderate statement of the issue would be more widely accepted, that while as interpreters we need all the help we can get from the historian, the text has to be read for itself and in itself.

While every scrap of external information is potentially valuable for interpretation of the OT, the surprising thing is how little is in reality significant. To understand Amos or Micah well, a paragraph or two of historical and social background probably suffices (and much more is largely guesswork); to interpret Jonah or Job it can hardly be necessary to learn about the historical origin of these books (valid though such an enquiry may be in itself), since we have no kind of certainty about such matters. To see the 'author's intention', indeed, can lead us no deeper into the meaning of these works than to ask directly about meaning, disregarding almost entirely questions of date and authorship except on the broadest scale. The vast bulk of the data we need for interpretation is contained in the works themselves.

*Engagement* The best interpreters of literary works are not usually those who lay claim to cool passionless detachment (which often means only the suppression of their more superficial prejudices) but those who care about the significance their interpretative work may have. Such engagement with the text does not imply any particular belief about whether the text is 'true' (whatever that may mean from time to time), but it implies concern with the question of its truth and a willingness and endeavour to reach a personal judgement. Students of Shakespeare, even at an elementary level, are called upon to discuss the character of Falstaff, the freedom or otherwise of Macbeth, the sincerity of Mark Antony, and in so doing they engage with the content of the text and with its 'truth'. And just as we may say in engaging with a fictional narrative, that it is 'true' or 'false' (or something in between), the same kind of judgements may be made of the biblical text – not indeed, with the claim of making a definitive assessment of the reality of the matter, but mainly in order to express one's own judgement of what is true or false. Genuine understanding requires evaluation; the interpreter's subjectivity is a proper element in the process of understanding, provided it does not dominate the process, and provided it allows itself to be open to correction or adjustment by the reality of the text.

The function of engagement and the process of developing understanding can be seen in any discussion of the ethics of the book of Proverbs. Suppose the question to be put is, whether the proverbs are fundamentally prudential or fundamentally religious – that is to say, are the readers of the book encouraged to follow its advice because they will benefit from it, or because its advice is God's will? It is not necessary to believe in the existence of God to engage with the question – indeed it is possible that a non-believer will argue the 'religious' interpretation while a believer will argue the 'prudential' interpretation (for, from a Christian point of view, for example, the religious element in Proverbs may seem decidedly weak). Engagement means that it matters to the interpreter how the issue is resolved, in that he or she has a personal stake in the issue. Prejudice would mean that we are concerned that the work be interpreted to suit the opinion we held before our work of interpretation began; engagement means that we are personally concerned with the content of the work and for that reason are concerned for its proper interpretation – at the very least, to know whether the work is a friend or a foe. Academic 'objectivity', as sometimes portrayed, would require rejection or suppression of one's legitimate interests and beliefs, and demand a concern only that the academic task be done well; engagement, which is no less steadfastly opposed to pure subjectivity and prejudice than is 'objectivity', takes seriously the human interpreter as part of the interpreting process, and sets up the business of understanding as a humanizing enterprise.

## Second-order methods

In this section I will consider methods in OT study that focus not upon texts in themselves, but upon texts in relation to other intellectual or political issues; their concern is not so much with understanding the biblical texts as with evaluating them from the standpoint of another commitment. Such an interest seems in principle to be perfectly legitimate; those with strong ethical views, for example about the equality of men and women, should be entitled to ask of the biblical texts how they measure up to the standards and values of our own age.

*Feminist criticism*    Feminist criticism can be seen as a paradigm for or exemplar of these evaluative criticisms. The starting point of feminist criticism is of course not the biblical texts themselves but the issues and concerns of feminism as a world view and as a political enterprise. We may describe feminism in general as the recognition that in the history of civilization women have been marginalized by men and have been denied access both to social positions of authority and influence, and to symbolic production (the creation of symbol systems, such as the making of texts, that influence ideas and behaviour). A feminist biblical criticism will therefore be concerned with exposing means or strategies by which women's subordination has been inscribed in and justified by those texts.

It is characteristic of feminist criticism to use a variety of approaches to literary texts and to encourage multiple readings. The idea that there is a 'proper' way to read texts is seen as a typical expression of traditional male control of texts and traditional male control of reading. Feminist biblical criticism sometimes concentrates on analysing from the evidence of the biblical texts how women's lives and voices in ancient Israel have in fact been suppressed by the texts, noticing how even women who are named in the OT are so rarely allowed to speak. At other times, feminist biblical criticism searches for traces of female interests in the biblical texts, which are on the whole, if not totally, androcentric. Some feminist biblical scholars think it is possible to discover within the OT texts, male-authored and male-centred as they are, much writing that is in fact pro-women and serviceable for feminists of today. Others are much less sanguine and think it their duty to expose the deep-seated sexism of the texts in the hope that women and men of our time may not automatically adopt the outlook of the Bible on gender issues, even if they are otherwise favourably disposed to the teachings of the Bible in general.

It can hardly be denied that the OT gives many messages to women, often subliminally, about what their ideals should be and how they should behave. Typically, the OT recognizes only two kinds of women: the good mother and the wicked seducer.

Women exist principally to produce children, especially male children; they are for the most part entirely subordinate to their menfolk. Even though they may have real power within the family context, they owe whatever authority they exercise to their fathers and husbands, and their place is firmly within the home. Women of today, if they read the Bible, have to be on their guard, so a feminist criticism claims, against adopting the women of the Bible as their role models.

In short, feminist biblical criticism, in whatever form it takes, adopts a stance toward the biblical texts that goes beyond mere understanding. While it is of course deeply concerned to understand what it is the Bible says about women and how in fact they are portrayed, its interest is rather more in evaluating, from a general feminist perspective, the biblical texts.

*Materialist or political criticism*   In materialist criticism, texts are viewed not primarily as expressions of ideas but principally as productions, as objects created, like other physical products, at a certain historical moment and within a particular social and economic setting. What is more, the biblical texts that we read today are not just fortunate survivors from the past that happen to be still available; rather, they have been kept alive by certain specific readerships, whether religious or literary, as well as by a publishing industry that finds it profitable to promote the book that is, after all, the world's best seller.

When it comes to the analysis of the biblical texts, what materialist criticism is interested in is the ways the texts served in the past and still serve today as vehicles for the use of power and in the interests of certain class or sectional groups. In ancient societies like Israel, as also in our own, there were rich and poor, people with power and those without; and materialist criticism seeks to identify whose interests a text served.

An example that can be taken of a materialist interpretation of a biblical text is that of the Ten Commandments. This text has usually been understood purely theologically – that is, as representing the will of God for human behaviour. A materialist criticism says that, whether or not that is the case, the Ten Commandments must have been promoted by some group in ancient Israelite society, for their own interests, and tries to identify who that group would have been. It is clear that those who need a law against theft are those with property to steal, and so on; and in fact, once we ask the question, Who is addressed in the commandments? it is not at all difficult to answer it in terms of class and gender. The Ten Commandments are evidently addressed to males, who are old enough to have sons and daughters and young enough to have living parents, who are men of property with houses and oxen and asses, who are men of standing in their community who can give true or false testimony in a law court, and so on. Other persons in the society, such as the young, the disabled, the foreign residents and women, are referred to but are not the subject of the laws; though some of the laws may benefit them, it is not for their sake that the laws have been created, but to sustain those who framed the laws in the positions of power they have become accustomed to.

Like feminist criticism, materialist criticism cannot do without a thorough understanding of the Hebrew Bible, but understanding is not its purpose. Its tendency or intention is to show that the biblical texts represent sectional interests and are not equally beneficial to all segments of Hebrew society. In so doing, materialist criticism tends to relativize the authority and continuing validity of the biblical texts, in stressing their human, and often all too human, origins.

*Reader-response criticism*   The outlook of this method or approach in biblical study is that it is the reader who is the creator of, or at the very least, an important contributor to, the meaning of texts. Reader-response critics do not think of 'meaning' as something that texts 'have', whether put there by an author (as in traditional historical criticism) or somehow existing intrinsically in the shape, structure and wording of the texts (as in rhetorical criticism). Rather, reader-response criticism regards meaning as coming into being at the meeting point of text and reader – or, in a more extreme form, as being actually created by readers in the act of reading.

It follows from this position that reader-response critics cannot speak of a text as having *a* meaning, a single, determinate meaning that we should as interpreters of the text be seeking to discover. 'Meaning' is what readers find in texts, what comes into readers' heads when they are reading texts. A text means whatever it means to its readers, no matter how strange or unacceptable some meanings may seem to other readers.

And if there is no single 'right' meaning of a text, no determinate meaning, it follows also that there are no intrinsically right or wrong interpretations. If the author cannot give validation to meanings and if the text itself is mute, the only source for validity in interpretation has to lie in 'interpretative communities' – groups that authorize certain meanings and disallow others. Such a group may be an academic community, which establishes norms by which it will allow certain interpretations and disallow others. Or it may be a church community, which will decide on what kinds of interpretations are suitable for its own purposes. Validity in interpretation is then recognized as relative to the group that authorizes it.

As an example of reader-response criticism we may take the story of the Flood. If we are reading it within the context of a community of religious belief, we may well want to regard it as a story of God's deliverance of the human race from a universal disaster – that is, as one of the mighty acts of God. But in another context, we might be able to read the story as a critique of God, whose creation of humans has apparently been so misguided that before very long he feels it necessary to wipe out the whole of humanity. Very few readers belong to just one reading community, of course, and what is most interesting about reader-response criticism is the interplay between different reading positions we can take up in the course of our study of the biblical texts.

*Deconstruction*   The 'common sense' assumption about texts and their meanings is that texts have more or less clear meanings and manage more or less successfully to convey those meanings to readers. That is, after all, the basis on which we read newspapers and novels and examination papers. But the philosophy of deconstruction is that, however true that may be in a practical sense, words and texts are ultimately inadequate for the tasks we put upon them, and inevitably undermine themselves, usually in a way that calls into question the ideas that the texts apparently exist to express. A text typically has a thesis to defend or a point of view to espouse; but inevitably texts falter and let slip evidence against their own cause. A text typically sets forth or takes for granted some set of oppositions, one term being privileged over its partner; but in so doing it cannot help allowing glimpses of the impossibility of sustaining those oppositions.

Here is an example of a self-deconstructing text. In Genesis 9, after the Flood is over, God gives to Noah a new set of commands for the age that will follow. Among them is the sentence, 'Whoever sheds the blood of a human, by a human shall that person's blood be shed' (v.6). At its face value, this is an authorization of capital punishment for the crime of murder, and it is no doubt, at the same time, the severest of warnings against committing the crime of murder. But in permitting or authorizing or demanding (whatever it is precisely that the verse does) that an act of murder be followed by an act of capital punishment, the command allows what it also prohibits: shedding the blood of another human. The text deconstructs itself by setting up an opposition between murder (bad) and capital punishment (good), and then undermining that distinction by giving the same name to the two acts: 'shedding the blood of a human'. If the two acts are the same, why should one be good and one be bad? The very way the text is formulated makes us wonder whether we would want to uphold the distinction between murder and capital punishment or whether we would want to call them both acts of murder, differing perhaps only in the fact that one is illegal (socially disapproved) and the other legal (socially approved).

Deconstruction, according to its practitioners, is not so much a method that can be applied to texts as an observation we can make about texts. Though a scholar may write a deconstructive essay about a text, it would be more correct to say that the scholar is showing how the text deconstructs itself than that the scholar has performed a deconstruction of the text. Deconstruction is an especially powerful tool in biblical study, in that it relativizes the authority attributed to biblical texts, and makes it evident that much of the power that is felt to lie in the texts is really the power of the community that supports them and sanctions them.

## Third-order methods

The three methods to be discussed under this heading are usually put on the same footing as those I have called 'first-order' methods. But the way I would distinguish the two groups is that the third-order methods principally *use* the biblical text for purposes beyond the text. This does not mean (i) that they do not incidentally shed valuable light on the text and so assist our interpretation of it, or (ii) that they are not legitimate subjects of study in their own right.

*Historical criticism*   A good deal of the OT is narrative of events; it is therefore a natural undertaking to examine how the narrated events correspond to what actually happened in history. Especially because much of the narrative concerns a nation and not just individuals, historians rightly regard the books of Samuel and Kings, for example, as providing the raw material for a reconstruction of Israel's history. And since the scholars best equipped to pursue such investigations are usually those who have been trained in biblical study and in OT interpretation, the impression is often given that historical study is a primary form of OT interpretation.

The term historical criticism refers to this enterprise of reconstructing the events lying behind the biblical narratives. But precisely because its focus is events and historical processes, its focus is not the biblical text and its goal cannot be the interpretation of the biblical text. Of course, everyone with an historical bent would like to know as well as possible what actually happened and would like to understand the factors behind the movements of history. But in that quest the OT becomes a source-book for the history; it is used as a tool, sometimes the best and sometimes only one among several, for reconstructing the past. In so far as historical criticism uses the biblical text, it is of course biblical study; but its contribution to biblical interpretation is usually indirect.

This is not to say that indirect contributions may not be very valuable. For example, every student of the OT who visits Israel and Jordan and travels through the land of the Bible finds that he or she has acquired an almost indelible perspective from which to read the OT. The gain is not quantifiable, and one's first-hand knowledge of topography is not likely to alter any OT interpretations (though it may help to preserve one from some errors). Historical reconstruction and synthesis will have a similar type of value. No doubt the story of the conflict between twelve young warriors of David and twelve of Ishbosheth at the pool in Gibeon (2Sam. 2.12–17) is illuminated if one knows that such a pool existed, and more so if one has stood by it oneself; but the meaning of the story is hardly touched by the historical reality. Or, to take a more significant example: suppose that historical research can show, as some contemporary historians believe, that the conquest of Canaan by the Israelite tribes was really an uprising of Canaanite peasants (perhaps incited by a small band of incoming Hebrews); what difference would that make to the understanding and interpretation of the biblical narratives of the 'conquest'? In one sense, a fundamental difference, in that these narratives would be shown to be only loosely connected with historical events; in other senses, none at all, since these narratives would continue to be tales about Israel's success when obedient to God, about Israel's unity, about leadership, about conflicts within and without a group, about religious war, and so on.

So while the results of historical criticism can be fed back into biblical study and determine one dimension of the biblical texts (their relationship to what happened), they do not generally have a decisive weight in their interpretation.

*Source criticism* This method seeks to reconstruct not the *events* that lie behind the OT texts, but the *sources* that lie behind their contents. Such sources were both written and oral, but the term 'source criticism' generally refers to the reconstruction of written sources. There can be no doubt that many of the biblical texts, especially narratives and laws, were derived or adapted from previously existing sources. Biblical writings very occasionally acknowledge their sources, as when a short poem on the 'standing still' of the sun in Joshua's time is followed by the comment, 'Is this not written in the Book of Jashar?' (Josh. 10.12–13; cf. Num. 21.14). More frequently, especially in Kings, reference is made to older books, now lost, where fuller detail was given (e.g. 1 Kings 11.41, 'Now the rest of the acts of Solomon . . . are they not written in the book of the acts of Solomon?'); it is a fair presumption that this was the source from which the author of Kings drew his material on Solomon. In the case of the Pentateuch, though there is no specific allusion to any of its major sources, it seems necessary to suppose a complicated history of older and younger sources from which the highly variegated complex of narrative, law and poetry was drawn.

It is sometimes supposed that the purpose of source criticism is to illuminate the final author's purpose by examining how he used his sources, what he omitted and what he retained, what he expanded or abbreviated, how he arranged the material available to him. But such studies, which we would today call redaction criticism, are rather rare compared with studies of the sources for their own sake, i.e. in order to discover what the sources were, and to arrange them in some sort of historical sequence, deciding which was the oldest and which drew upon which. And studies of the author's use of his sources can only be effective to the extent with which we have sure knowledge of the contents of his sources.

Thus within biblical studies generally the most successful application of source criticism to interpretation has been in the Synoptic Gospels – so long, that is, as it has been widely accepted that Mark was a source of Matthew and Luke. In the OT, the postulated four major sources of the Pentateuch, J E D P, are (unlike Mark) not extant, though to many scholars' satisfaction they can be reconstructed with detailed accuracy. Surprisingly, however, very few scholars have used this reconstruction of the sources as a means for interpreting the text that now stands. Generally speaking, the goal of source criticism has been the sources themselves, their contents, historical settings, purposes and interrelationships.

If we imagine the direction of source criticism changing, or of source criticism being absorbed into redaction criticism, we can conceive how source criticism could be deployed in the service of interpreting the literary works we now have. But even so, it needs to be said that many of the certainties among former generations of source critics are now increasingly called into question; and if we cannot now find agreement on the profiles of J E D and P, we are so much further from using them to interpret the Pentateuch in its final form.

Perhaps the most satisfying application of source criticism in OT studies has been in the discrimination between source material and editorial material in the Deuteronomistic History. Here it is not so much the detection of the historian's sources that is valuable for interpreting his work, but the isolation of those passages in which he is not following any source but freely composing and therefore expressing his own ideas and theological outlook.

*Form criticism*   While historical criticism attempts to reach behind the biblical text to reconstruct the history of Israel, form criticism reaches back to the oral folk literature of Israel. Its principles are these: that embedded in the written literature of a people are samples of their earlier oral literature, and that many literary forms (legends, hymns, laments, and so on) had in the oral stage a particular function in the life of the people (a life-setting; German *Sitz im Leben*). In gospel studies, form criticism sought to recover the early Christian preaching in which the narratives of Jesus' sayings and acts were recounted and took on fixed shapes. In OT studies, form criticism was fruitfully applied to the Psalms, each type of psalm (thanksgiving by an individual, hymn of praise, appeal by the community, etc.) being shown to belong to a certain type of occasion in Israelite worship. Narratives were also designated as 'aetiological saga' (a tale purporting to account for the origins of a custom or a place), 'legend' (a tale about a holy man, holy place or sacred custom that points a moral), and so on.

Form criticism performs a valuable service in its concern with classifying types of literature within the biblical texts (e.g. prose and poetry and their subdivisions). By enquiring after the typical it highlights what is individual in any piece of literature, and by identifying the type or genre of the passage in question (as hymn, prophetic speech, instruction, family saga, for example) it offers a major interpretative key to the passage. (We would be hard pressed to interpret the story in Judg. 9.8–15 about the trees' attempt to anoint a king over them until we recognized that it was a 'fable'!) But in that it attempts to reconstruct the roles the OT literature played in the life of Israel, its goal is not the interpretation as such of the biblical text.

It is as well to bear in mind also the provisional (not to say speculative) nature of much form criticism, as well as of much source criticism. This is no objection to these disciplines as such, but merely a reminder that in the field of the humanities knowledge does not have the precision that some scholars give the air of having achieved. In part our lack of precision is a defect due largely to the rather fragmentary nature of our subject matter; in part, however, it is a blessing, in that it gives room for individual perception, accords insight a higher value than labour, and engages the interpreter, whether novice or expert, as a person in the process of interpretation.

Throughout, this chapter has not been purely *descriptive* of the methods employed in OT studies, but has attempted also to be partly *prescriptive*. The arrangement of the chapter, and especially the division into 'first-order', 'second-order' and 'third-order' methods, reflects a deliberate re-evaluation of current methods. Students, beginning and more advanced, may find it of interest to consider to what extent their own courses of study appear to reflect the hierarchy of methods outlined in this chapter.

47

## FURTHER READING

GENERAL

John Barton, *Reading the Old Testament: Method in Biblical Study* (London, Darton, Longman & Todd, 1984).

J. Cheryl Exum and David J.A. Clines (eds.), *The New Literary Criticism and the Hebrew Bible* (Journal for the Study of the Old Testament Supplement Series, 143; Sheffield, JSOT Press, 1993).

Terence J. Keegan, *Interpreting the Bible: A Popular Introduction to Biblical Hermeneutics* (New York, Paulist Press, 1985).

Richard N. Soulen, *Handbook of Biblical Criticism* (Atlanta, John Knox Press, 1976).


SPECIFIC

David J.A. Clines, *What Does Eve Do to Help? and Other Readerly Questions to the Old Testament* (Journal for the Study of the Old Testament Supplement Series, 94; Sheffield, JSOT Press, 1990).

— *Interested Parties: The Ideology of Writers and Readers of the Hebrew Bible* (Journal for the Study of the Old Testament Supplement Series, 105; Gender, Culture, Theory, 1; Sheffield, Sheffield Academic Press, 1995).

Norman C. Habel, *Literary Criticism of the Old Testament* (Philadelphia, Fortress Press, 1971).

Gene M. Tucker, *Form Criticism of the Old Testament* (Philadelphia, Fortress Press, 1971).

# 3

## Old Testament History and the History of Israel

### JOHN ROGERSON

Until recently, Old Testament historical traditions were studied with the help of modern textbooks such as J. Bright's *A History of Israel* (1981)[1] or Martin Noth's *The History of Israel* (1958).[2] Of the two, Bright's was by far the more traditional, and followed the OT order of Patriarchs, Exodus, Settlement, Judges, Monarchy, Exile and Restoration. Noth's was more radical in that it began with the Settlement in Canaan, and treated the material about the Patriarchs and the Exodus as traditions expressing Israel's belief about its past rather than as data that could be used to reconstruct that past historically.

In the last ten years or so, the situation has altered so radically that, at the time of writing, there is no textbook in English on the history of Israel that presents an up-to-date picture of the state of scholarship in this field. The reason for the change is that what used to be called 'biblical archaeology' has been superceded by archaeological investigation that is less willing to accept the historical traditions of the OT as the framework in which to set archaeological discoveries. This, in turn, reflects a general movement within archaeology to distrust written sources, and is thus not a specific attack on the OT. Some of the many archaeological findings that have begun to emerge can be summarized as follows.

Towards the end of the Late Bronze Age (fourteenth century BCE) there was a noticeable decrease in the number of occupied sites in ancient Palestine. It is assumed that, for reasons unknown, there was a movement of population to northern Trans-Jordan, where people became semi-sedentary, before beginning to move back to Palestine in the second half of the

49

thirteenth century. The increase in settled and new sites is very marked, with occupation beginning in the more fertile eastern and central valleys of the Bethel and Samaria hills, and spreading slowly during the following decades to the western parts. The area of Judah seems not to have been resettled in the same way. From these settlers there emerged in due course small 'states' – the northern kingdom of Israel in the ninth century and the southern kingdom of Judah a little later. Similar developments took place at the same time in Trans-Jordan in the areas of Ammon, Moab and Edom.

The main result of these findings is to set a large question mark against the biblical account of the reigns of David and Solomon, with their picture of a small Israelite empire ruled from Jerusalem in the tenth century that included the states of Edom, Ammon and Moab. This, in turn, has undermined an assumption that long shaped views on OT history, namely that Solomon created a scribal bureaucracy to administer his empire, and that it was this scribal bureaucracy that began to collect and write down the stories of the Patriarchs and the Exodus, etc. If Judah, for example, did not become a small state until the eighth century, and if the recording of her history began only then, how much can be known about her past? One view is that nothing can be known about ancient Israel's history before the exile; but this is too extreme. Israelite kings such as Omri and Jehu of the ninth century, and Judahite kings such as Uzziah, Ahaz and Hezekiah of the eighth century are attested in Assyrian records. However, whether very much can be said with confidence about the period prior to, say, the time of Omri, is a matter of keen debate.

For beginning students, such radical conclusions about OT history can be very disturbing, especially as it is popularly supposed that archaeology has proved the Bible to be historically true. There is also the fact, discussed in Chapter 1, that critical scholarship has accepted for over a hundred years that the actual history of Israel's religion differed radically from the surface story given in the OT.

The difficulties felt by beginners are usually theological in origin. If they have been taught that the Bible is the word of God, or inspired, they will wonder how it can be that scholars approach its history in such a radical way. Yet it is possible to adopt a radical approach to Israel's history while at the same time valuing the OT historical traditions as expressions, through the medium of history writing, of prophetic faith and hope. Two things need to be done. First, the nature of modern historical method has to be understood. Second, the purpose of the OT historical traditions has to be considered.

In any use of the historical method today, the cross-checking of sources for evidence is an essential part of the procedure. The fact is that memories are not always reliable. It is well known that eye-witness accounts of campaigns in the Second World War by generals who fought them are not always accurate when checked against official communiqués or telegrams or reports of the period. Further, when modern historians piece together a narrative on the basis of information that may have gaps, they have to make guesses. Discoveries subsequent to their work may show the guesses to have been incorrect. If to remember incorrectly is a sign of incompetence or dishonesty, then many distinguished generals have been incompetent or dishonest. If to make guesses about what happened in history, guesses which are later shown to have been incorrect, is a sign of incompetence or of dishonesty, then many historians, including historians who have tried to reconstruct the history of Israel, have been incompetent or dishonest. In fact, anyone who is engaging in the serious writing of history is taking the risk of making mistakes.

There is a further important point to make here. When later historians correct the work of earlier historians, they do not necessarily show themselves to be 'better' historians. A nineteenth-century historian may have worked only from medieval manuscripts that were preserved in libraries all over Europe that, well before the days of photocopying, had to be visited. A present-day historian may benefit from having a book or books in which all those manuscripts plus several that have come to light more recently are reproduced, together with commentaries and critical notes written by experts. Just because modern historians possess far more sources of information than did historians of one hundred years ago, it does not follow that they are 'better' than their nineteenth-century counterparts. Nineteenth-century historians may have possessed a much sounder historical judgement, and greater flair for writing historical narrative than their modern counterparts.

Similarly, when modern scholars produce reconstructions of biblical history that differ from what the Bible says, they are not showing themselves to be 'better' than the biblical authors. The modern scholar has available many aids that were unknown to the biblical writer. For example, the modern scholar possesses historical records of the empires of Assyria and Babylon from the ninth to the sixth centuries BCE. These are centuries during which life in Israel and Judah was dominated by the expansion of these empires towards and into Syria and Palestine. It is no exaggeration to say that modern scholarship knows far more about that part of the ancient world in which the Hebrew people lived than the Hebrews could ever have known themselves. This in no way makes modern scholars superior to biblical writers. They are, rather, grateful for the opportunity to study the OT in the light of such enlarged knowledge.

At this point it is worth considering what we can guess about how the biblical authors wrote their histories. As stated earlier, it has become problematic to assume that Solomon set up a rudimentary civil service to administer his empire, and that the beginnings of OT history writing began under Solomon in the tenth century. However, conditions for history writing certainly existed in Judah by the time of Hezekiah (727–698 BCE), and the destruction of the northern kingdom of Israel by the Assyrians in 722/1 BCE and the influx of refugees from the north into Jerusalem at that time provided the impulse for recording the past history of Judah and Israel.

The history that was written was based mainly upon brief administrative and financial records kept both in Samaria and Jerusalem. Whether there were fuller accounts such as the 'Chronicles of the Kings of Judah and Israel', which are mentioned in the books of Kings as sources, we do not know. Nor do we know how far back the story of Israel's past was taken. There *could* at this stage (late eighth century BCE) have been a continuous story running from the Patriarchs to the time of Hezekiah, but we cannot be sure of this. If there was such a story, it drew upon traditions about great ancestors from the stories of the Patriarchs, with the Judahite ancestor Abraham connected with Hebron preceding the Israelite hero Jacob, who was connected with Bethel. Other popular stories about local heroes were used to construct the period of the Judges, in which it was assumed that twelve judges had ruled consecutively in the period between Joshua and the first king Saul. The date of the stories about Saul, David and Solomon is much disputed, with some authorities maintaining that they were composed after the exile. While it is certain that it was only after the exile that all the traditions in Genesis, Exodus, Numbers, Judges, Samuel and Kings reached their final form, it is going too far to suggest that figures such as Samuel, Saul, David and Solomon never existed. There are elements in the traditions about them that cannot simply be explained by later invention, for all that the stories in their final form probably reflect the interests of much later periods.

For the period after 560 BCE, the biblical writers were worse off for sources than they had been for the history of the previous four hundred years. A probable reason for this is that Jerusalem was no longer an administrative capital where records were kept. Judah was part of a province governed from Samaria or Rabbat Ammon. Apart from the personal recollections of Nehemiah (which, like all personal recollections, may not always have been objective), who was appointed governor of Judah by Artaxerxes I in 445 BCE, historical allusions to the period 519–516 BCE in the prophetic books of Haggai and Zechariah 1–8, and extracts from official Persian records in the book of Ezra, there was little to go on. In describing the work of Ezra, the biblical writers may have drawn extensively upon what Nehemiah claims to have done. This would be reasonable, given the belief of the biblical writers that Ezra and Nehemiah were roughly contemporary. The authors of the Books of Chronicles wrote a history covering the period from the time of Saul (I Chron. 10) to the return from exile (539 BCE) from a priestly point of view. They probably used as a source the Books of Samuel and Kings, together with supplementary material whose origin is unclear and whose reliability is a matter of debate.

This brief attempt to consider what historical resources were available to the biblical writers and how they might have used them may serve two purposes. First, it may help us to appreciate that the histories in the OT came into being in much the same way as all histories do: by the collecting of sources and the writing of historical accounts on their basis. Second, it may help to bridge the cultural gap that exists between ourselves and the OT period.

I have been insisting that although the biblical writers had far fewer resources than we enjoy, and did not have the sense of critical evaluation of evidence that we have developed comparatively recently, none the less they were not acting differently from us in principle. I propose to develop this with regard to the idea of history as explanation.

One of the tasks of the modern historian is to explain a state of affairs by giving an account of what led up to it. Why did Britain declare war on Germany in September 1939? One answer is because Germany did not reply to the British demand to cease hostilities against Poland. However, this cannot be seen in isolation from what preceded it, at least as far back as the end of the First World War and possibly even the Franco-Prussian war of 1871. Thus a modern historian may present an account that, beginning with the 1914–18 war, explains and leads up to the German invasion of Poland, the immediate cause of the British declaration of war in 1939.

In the OT we find similar attempts to explain a situation in terms of what preceded it. Why was Jerusalem destroyed by the Babylonians in 587 BCE? One answer is that Zedekiah, whom Nebuchadnezzar put on the throne when he first captured Jerusalem in 597, rebelled against his overlord. However, this is not the whole story, and it is one of the purposes of the Books of Kings to explain the fall of Jerusalem by describing what, over many centuries, led up to the events of 587.

But at this point there is a most significant difference between the biblical account and what a modern historian would attempt. The biblical writer describes the events that led up to the fall of Jerusalem in 587 in order to indicate that it was the punishment of God upon his people. Some modern historians might attribute the fall of a nation to its moral laxity; none would attempt to explain it in terms of a divine purpose. It could be argued that the reason for this difference was that the biblical writers were unaware of secular forces such as economic or political pressures, and that they tended to attribute everything to God. We must notice, however, that at the time of the fall of Jerusalem there was another factor present that modern historians would regard as quite outside their terms of reference: a prophetic factor.

During the siege of Jerusalem, the prophet Jeremiah main-tained that the city would fall, and that only surrender to the enemy would save it. God, declared Jeremiah, was on the side of the Babylonians fighting against the city that was believed by its inhabitants to enjoy God's special protection. This preaching of Jeremiah brought threats against his life, and only with difficulty did he survive to witness what he had proclaimed. Among his opponents had been other prophets who had forecast victory for Judah. The explanation of the fall of Jerusalem in the Books of Kings in terms of what led up to it is also a prophetic inter-pretation – an interpretation based upon the insights of a tiny group of people who stood in an intimate relationship to God that was often terrifying for themselves and embarrassing for their hearers. It would be wrong to suggest that *all* history writing in the OT is as closely bound up with prophetic witness as is the fall of Jerusalem with Jeremiah. But this particular example indicates at its sharpest the real difference between biblical history and modern history. The latter would regard interpretation of events in terms of divine intention as outside its terms of reference.

What is true of modern historians is true also of biblical scholars. They do not claim to have *prophetic* insight into why events took place as they did in OT times. If they are convinced that they can reconstruct the course of events with more accuracy than did the biblical writers, they know that they can never be in a position to make judgements about the claim of the biblical writers that they could discover a divine intention in a pattern of events.

But this brings us to a very serious question that may not only worry beginners in OT studies, but that certainly divides even critical scholars. If biblical writers could have been wrong about the exact sequence of events, how can we take seriously their claim to discover a divine purpose in them? If the events did not happen, or happened differently from how the biblical writers believed, how can there have been a divine intention in them?

In trying to answer this, we must distinguish between at least two possible ways in which divine intention might be discerned in events: the direct and the indirect. A good example of the direct would be Jeremiah's involvement in the fall of Jerusalem. There was nothing built into the complex of events that we call the fall of Jerusalem that indicated irresistibly that it was God's will that the city should fall. Jeremiah's witness to this effect was not well received. But he was directly involved in the events, and declared with prophetic conviction what he believed to be their significance from God's point of view.

By the indirect way of discerning divine intention, I mean the possibility that people far removed in time from the events they were considering, and dependent upon oral or written traditions, could see a pattern in the events that suggested a divine intention. They might then so edit, or arrange, the materials as to emphasize that divine intention. In so doing, they might be dependent upon information that was in part unreliable, though they would not know that it was unreliable. They might introduce what the modern scholar would see as distortions, although they would not be aware that they were deliberately distorting anything. Thus, paradoxical as it might seem, it is possible to accept that compared with modern historical reconstruction, OT accounts of happenings may contain inaccuracies, but that this does not invalidate the OT claim to have discerned a divine intention in the events.

Put into other words, modern historical study of the OT is not an attack upon the integrity of the biblical writers. It does not set out from the assumption that everything in the OT is false unless it can be proved to be true. If critical scholars come to the conclusion that the course of events was not as presented in the OT, this is because they have access to materials and methods not known to the OT writers. If the beginner can come to terms with this, then he or she will have negotiated one of the most difficult stumbling blocks to serious OT study.

To sum up this chapter: the OT does not contain the history of ancient Israel. It contains historical and story-like traditions whose primary purpose is to express the faith of the authors of the OT that God had been involved in the events of Israelite history. This material *can* be used by modern scholarship to reconstruct the history of Israel, in conjunction with texts and archaeological findings from the ancient world.

The history of Israel, as reconstructed by a modern scholar, can shed light on parts of the OT. There are historical events that are alluded to in prophetic books, but not mentioned elsewhere in the OT. For example, Isaiah 20.1–6 is probably to be connected with a revolt by Judah and other small states against Assyria in 713–711 BCE; but this revolt is only known to us from sources outside the OT. Again, we know more about King Omri than the OT tells us in I Kings 16, since he is mentioned in several extra-biblical sources. These latter give us an idea of the immense political and economic skill of Omri, a king who took over a weak and divided country and rapidly transformed it into the most powerful small kingdom in the region. It is all the more remarkable that the biblical writer deals with him in a few verses, and comments primarily on the fact that, from the religious viewpoint, he was a very evil king.

Scholars who write a *History of Israel*, or who lecture on the subject, are not producing something that is intended to replace the historical traditions of the OT. They are not writing their own versions of the OT. Indeed, their reconstructions will need to be corrected and improved in the light of further research.

The historical traditions of the OT can never be replaced, because they are part of a witness to faith in the God of Israel, faith that arose in deeply religious circles in ancient Israel. Their primary purpose is not to provide source material for modern historians but to express faith in the God of Israel. Nothing that critical scholarship can do to the OT can call into question the fact that this faith in God existed, and was expressed in the OT historical traditions. The existence of this witness to faith is a challenge to the faith, or lack of it, of today's world. It is possible both to acknowledge that challenge, and to treat the traditions in which it is expressed, honestly and critically.

## NOTES

1  J. Bright, *A History of Israel* (3rd edn London, SCM, 1981; Philadelphia, Westminster, 1981).
2  M. Noth, *The History of Israel* (2nd edn London, Black, 1972; New York, Harper, 1960).

# 4

## The World-View of the
## Old Testament

### JOHN ROGERSON

In the preface to this book, it was stated that the essays hoped to fulfil the same role in relation to the Old Testament as a travel guide does when you visit a foreign country. This is especially true of the present chapter. The people of the OT used a language very different from our own. They lived in an area of different climate and terrain compared with our own. Above all, they lived a very long time ago – roughly 3,700 to 2,100 years ago. Although, thanks to modern discoveries, we know a great deal about the ancient Near or Middle East, we must avoid two extremes in considering how ancient Israelites saw and responded to the world. On the one hand, we must not exaggerate the differences between them and modern western people, with the result that we create an uncrossable gulf. On the other hand, we must not imagine that the cultural differences were slight and unimportant. It is a fact that even if we have little knowledge of the cultural conditions of ancient Israel, much of the OT is still perfectly intelligible. But greater knowledge of the cultural background brings appreciation of points that would otherwise be missed.

This chapter will deal with the world of nature, magic, miracles, sacrifice and social organization. However, a word of introduction to these separate treatments is necessary.

In the chapter on the individual and the community, Paul Joyce warns against making generalizations about ancient Israelites, especially about how they thought. He rightly points to the diversity to be found in the OT. In this chapter, it will be impossible to avoid the impression that his warnings are being ignored. What this chapter attempts to describe, however, is not an entity that can be labelled 'the ancient Israelite mind'. Rather, the intention is to present something of the general framework, or shared cultural assumptions, within which the diversity of Israelite thinking took place.

The big difference between ancient Israelites and ourselves lay in the way boundaries were drawn. For example, we make no distinctions between 'clean' and 'unclean' birds, animals and sea creatures. In the OT, this is a most important distinction. Not only does it regulate what may and may not be eaten; it regulates what may and may not be sacrificed. But it goes further than this. It is part of a way of looking at the natural world that divides that world into definite spheres. In Genesis chapter 1, these spheres are identified as sky, land and sea, each with creatures appropriate to the sphere. There is some evidence that the 'unclean' creatures do not fit exactly into any sphere. For example, locusts fly but have four legs (cf. Leviticus 11.20). It is not possible to explain all the unclean creatures in this way, but there can be no doubt that the distinction between clean and unclean creatures reflects shared Israelite assumptions about order in the world of nature, and that by observing rules about contact with clean and unclean creatures, Israelites were ordering their lives in conformity with a coherent set of symbols.

As will be pointed out in the section on sacrifice, the distinction between clean and unclean is at the heart of the way in which boundaries were established in what we would call the moral and ritual spheres. The purpose of sacrifice was to enable those boundaries to be crossed when occasion demanded – for example, when a person became a priest and thus became identified with the realm of the 'holy' – and for the boundaries to be restored when they had been violated. It is probable that ancient Israelites were much more conscious than we are about the importance of different roles in society, and that boundaries between roles were clearly marked. It is difficult to know what the coronation of a monarch signifies in modern societies where there are still monarchs (e.g. in Britain). Perhaps such ceremonies are simply opportunities to indulge in pageantry and merry-making. It is likely that in ancient Israel a coronation played a much more definite role in placing the monarch in that sphere of reality that belonged properly only to monarchs. In the sphere of the family and of social relationships, Israelites were undoubtedly much more aware than we are of the network of kinship relationships in which they were located. In a society where the enforcement of law and order was often a local matter, the responsibility of the family or of the 'tribe', it was necessary to know who were one's kin and who were one's potential enemies. It was necessary to know on whom to rely for support in the event of conflicts between larger social units. In other words, it was necessary to be aware of boundaries separating friend and foe, and of boundaries enclosing relatives of nearer or remoter kinship. Genealogies, of which the OT seems to contain many, were important here, although it is probable that the OT in fact has only a small proportion of the genealogies that must have existed. Genealogies achieved at least two things. First, they helped to mark which social groups were linked politically, and which could therefore rely on each other for aid (with the implication that to mark allies is also to make it clear who are potential enemies). Second, they could establish rights of individuals or of families to residence in particular places, or of access to particular lands or wells.

Not only were the worlds of nature and social relationships clearly marked by boundaries. So was the world of time. It is no accident that Genesis 1 describes the creation of the luminaries whose function is not only to separate day from night, but to be 'for times and seasons and for days and years' (Gen. 1.14). The observance of festivals of the new moon (1 Samuel 20.5ff.) and of the sabbath, not to mention the great festivals of the agricultural year, divided time clearly between the sacred and the ordinary. Indeed, the purpose of all the boundaries, wherever they were set up, was to order the whole of life in regard to the distinction between sacred and ordinary. Israelites who had proper regard for the boundaries could be sure that their lives and those of their families were ordered according to the will of God. When boundaries were transgressed, means were provided of restoring them.

The attempt has been made here to present a picture of order – albeit a very different type of order compared with what we are used to. It is necessary to make a few remarks about discussions about ancient Israelites that appear to give the opposite impression, suggesting that Israelites lived in a somewhat mystical world in which they were unable to make some of the distinctions that are fundamental to our perception of life. In a separate chapter Paul Joyce discusses the concept of 'corporate personality', according to which Israelites could not distinguish clearly between the individual and the group to which they belonged. The purpose of the sections on magic and on miracles in the present chapter is to combat the views, first, that Israelites and their neighbours were so unscientific that they thought that any thing could influence any other similar thing (e.g. if they had the colour yellow in common), and second, that being incapable of distinguishing between what we would call normal and extra-ordinary events (miracles), they could see any happening in the world of nature as a divine event, and thus had a view of nature as a 'thou' rather than as an 'it'.[1] The view of the present chapter is that Israelites were well aware of the difference between ordinary and extra-ordinary events, that nature was not capable of producing a miracle at any moment, and that access to God was not the result of a mystical perception of reality, but was mediated by the boundaries that were clearly marked in the realms of nature, morality, social organization and role, and times and seasons.

## *The world of nature*

Israelite experience of the world of nature was considerably affected by the variations in terrain and climate to be found within ancient Israel. For example, Jerusalem is on the eastern edge of a zone that stretches to the west as far as Spain, and that contains Mediterranean fauna and flora. Yet only about a mile to the east of Jerusalem there begins a treeless wilderness, which in turn becomes desert, dropping down to over 1,000 feet below sea level at the Dead Sea. The rift valley in which the Dead Sea is found shares fauna and flora with such places as the east of the Sudan. Only six miles to the east of Jerusalem, the rainfall is less than eight inches a year – insufficient for wheat to be grown. The agricultural implications of such variations will be obvious.[2] However, ancient Israelites were aware not only of agricultural implications of the very different types of land to which they were used. In the boundaries that they drew in order to demarcate reality, they regarded the uncultivable lands with suspicion. They belonged to the sphere of the chaotic and disordered, peopled by wild animals and demons. Humans who lived there, or who were exiled there, were not members of an ordered society.

In Jerusalem and the hill country on which it stands, rainfall was vital for the farmer. Yet it varied considerably, and there could be years of low rainfall, permitting only very poor crops. When there was very high rainfall, as seems to be the case in modern Israel every twelve years or so, this could do more harm than good. Although the land promised to the ancient Israelites is described in the OT as flowing with milk and honey (Exodus 3.8), it is clear from the OT that nature was a hard taskmaster. We are told that Abram (Genesis 12) and Elimelech (Ruth 1) were forced to leave their homes because of famine. The seven fat and seven lean years in Egypt, familiar from the story of Joseph (Genesis 37, 39–47), produced a famine in Canaan, with the result that Joseph's brothers were forced to travel to Egypt to buy grain. In 1 Kings 17–18 we find descriptions of the terrible effects of a drought that lasted for several years. Agriculture could also be affected by blight and mildew (Amos 4.9) or by a plague of locusts (Joel 2.1–9). When rain came after a drought, it could cause severe damage. The NT saying of Jesus about the wise and foolish builders suggests the effects of storms and floods after a period of drought, when the earth would be no more receptive to the rains than concrete.

Because imports enable us to eat almost whatever we like all the year round, quite apart from the fact that they cushion us against the effects of bad harvests, we must not forget that in ancient Israel crops and fruits were available only in season, and then only in quantities determined by the success or otherwise of the harvest. Grain could be stored, but usually only in sufficient quantity to guarantee a supply for the year. The grain harvest was in April–May, while in September–October there was the fruit harvest. Like their neighbours, ancient Israelites were deeply dependent upon the yearly cycle of nature. But unlike their neighbours, they celebrated the various significant points of the yearly cycle in terms of their belief and traditions about God's saving actions on their behalf, and his demands upon them as his people. Thus the fruit harvest was linked to traditions about God's provision for his people when they passed through the wilderness on their way from Egypt to the promised land (Leviticus 23.39–43). The first fruits of the harvests were offered back to God as a recognition that his was the land and that he was the provider. This, of course, is the idealized view of later tradition. Actual practice no doubt varied.

It is probable that when Israelites contemplated nature, they were made aware of the sublime: of that which was so exalted or impressive as to inspire awe and wonder. When the OT talks about God in relation to nature, it often emphasizes awe-inspiring phenomena.

The voice of the LORD breaks the cedars . . .
The voice of the LORD flashes forth flames of fire.
The voice of the LORD shakes the wilderness . . .
The voice of the LORD makes the oaks to whirl, and strips
the forests bare . . .
The LORD sits enthroned over the flood (Psalm 29.5–10
RSV)

When I look at thy heavens, the work of thy fingers, the moon
and the stars which thou hast established;
What is man that thou art mindful of him, and the son of man
that thou dost care for him? (Psalm 8.3–4 RSV)

The failure of the rains or of the harvest, and natural disasters
such as earthquakes (Amos 1.1) or floods, were obviously a
source of great concern to the Israelites. For the OT writers,
because such failures or disasters pointed to the sublime, to that
which inspired awe and wonder, they were indications of God's
judgement upon the people (cf. Amos 4.6–13). This view was not
always shared, however, by the ordinary people. They tended to
turn to the religion of their neighbours, a religion that was
closely bound up with the yearly cycle and that sought to
influence the natural processes by magico-religious ceremonies
so that agricultural prosperity would be ensured. The result was
a clash between prophetic religion and that of the ordinary
people, sometimes supported by the monarch. 1 Kings 18
provides us with a striking story of such a clash, in which the
prophets of Baal, who had the support of the Queen, were
confronted by Elijah. At issue was which God was the most
powerful, and which God should have the loyalty of the people.
Some passages in the OT, for example Psalm 104, seem to
suggest that the Israelites saw God as directly involved in all the
processes of the natural world. However, it would be unwise to
regard texts such as Psalm 104 as evidence for how Israelites
perceived reality. As has been pointed out earlier, they probably
saw the natural world as divided up into distinct ordered
spheres, and they approached God in ordered ways believed to
be prescribed by him. Psalm 104 is a religious text expressing
faith in God as the creator and sustainer. It is no more a guide to
general thought processes than are modern hymns.
An important point that should be made is that it was not
always easy for faith in God as creator and sustainer to be

maintained in OT times. Many of the ordinary people turned to other forms of religion because it was thought that these gave a more coherent account of life. Whatever else it was, faith in God in the OT was not a conclusion, drawn from an allegedly benign and orderly universe, that this universe must have an originator. OT faith in God was based upon an initiative of God into the affairs of his people that required faith that God was the creator and sustainer – even if there was much that seemed to count against this faith.

## *Magic*

The type of religion to which many of the ordinary people of Israel turned, and that was condemned by the prophets, is usually described as involving magic. As stated above, it was closely associated with the yearly cycle of nature, and it was designed to achieve agricultural prosperity. It involved what is often called imitative magic – the attempt to obtain the desired results by imitating those results in advance. Thus, the limping dances performed by the prophets of Baal in their encounter with Elijah on Mount Carmel (1 Kings 18.26) may have been attempts to imitate the descent of fire. Or the sacred prostitution denounced by the prophets (Hosea 2.2ff.) may have been an attempt to stimulate or imitate the creative processes of nature. There is even an example of an Israelite prophet using apparent imitative magic, on the occasion on which Elisha instructed King Joash to fire arrows into the ground. The king fired only three times, and the prophet was annoyed. The arrows were victories over Syria, and the three firings would mean only three victories. Had the king fired more times, he would have won sufficient victories to defeat Syria permanently (2 Kings 13.14–19).

Because of the largely negative attitude towards non-Israelite religion and its magical elements in the OT, to write a section about magic is to discuss part of the hidden agenda of the OT. Yet some explanation is called for. Magic is often thought to be an indication of a primitive and non-scientific world-view. If people think that sacred prostitution will help crops to grow, what sort of a world do they live in? It is true that magic betrays a view of the world in which scientific knowledge is much more meagre than in the modern world; but it would be wrong to suppose that because people try to obtain results by imitation, they live in a chaotic and disordered universe where anything that has something in common with something else can affect it.[3]

Magic must be set in the context of the boundaries that this chapter has been trying to describe. It comes into its own in situations where the boundaries are breached or blurred. For example, to be involved with the death of a member of a family is to find oneself in a boundary situation, that between life and death, and magical rites are used in many 'simple' societies in such cases. Sickness is another case where the boundary between life and death may be seen to be threatened, and where magic may be used. Since the provision of a food supply is of immense importance for the well-being and survival of a community, magic can be used in this circumstance also.

Those who take part in magico-religious ceremonies must not be thought of as simply trying to manipulate reality in a pseudo-scientific way. The people concerned do not neglect to carry out to the full the practical skills necessary to what they are doing. Hunters do not neglect to maintain their weapons and to keep watch over their trails; farmers do not cease to care for their soils. Without doubt, those who perform actions that imitate or symbolize what they hope to achieve believe that there is a better chance of success than if they did not perform the symbolic actions. This, in turn, may release them from anxiety, and help them to go more effectively about their business.

It cannot be stressed too strongly that in societies such as those found among Israel's neighbours, magico-religious ceremonies were essentially corporate. In a situation in which the very great majority of the people were engaged in agriculture, there was a much greater awareness of the interrelatedness of the social and the natural worlds than we can possibly appreciate, unless we have been brought up in a small agricultural community. The failure of crops, or unseasonal weather, was not simply the concern of farmers who would complain whatever the weather was like. It was the concern of the whole community.

The magico-religious acts that were performed in connection with the cycle of the agricultural year served to bind the people together, in harmony and hope, in the execution of their agricultural tasks. The ceremonies expressed and reinforced shared beliefs, and helped the people to go about their work in the context of a view of life that made sense to them. When, as often, the crops failed, this must have disturbed the more thoughtful among the people at the intellectual level. But nothing short of a major upheaval would undermine the general conviction that it was necessary to go on carrying out the magico-religious ceremonies. Magic does not suggest a chaotic view of the world. On the contrary, it functions within the order provided by many boundaries, and it can only be got rid of by the total destruction of those boundaries and the provision of alternative ones.

The opposition of the OT writers to the practices of Israel's neighbours to which the ordinary people turned was not an opposition merely to magical ceremonies as such. It was opposition to the way in which these ceremonies interpreted the boundaries of life as a whole. In the interpretation of the boundary between ruler and ruled, and between powerful and weak, the religion of Israel's neighbours knew little of the demands of the God of Israel that the strong should defend and preserve the weak. Also, aspects of the religion of Israel's neighbours, such as sacred prostitution, were repugnant to the OT writers.

The OT writers were not saying to the ordinary people: you must carry out your work of agriculture and trust in God rather than in magic. They were warning against total commitment to the interpretation of life that willingness to share in magico-religious ceremonies involved. It is only when we understand the magical component of the religion of Israel's neighbours in this way that we shall appreciate the threat it constituted to the religion of Israel, and the vehemence with which it was denounced not only by the prophets, but in the commands in the books of Deuteronomy and Joshua that the Israelites should utterly destroy their Canaanite neighbours lest they be persuaded to serve their gods.

## Miracles

The view of God of the OT writers is that he is the creator and the lord of the world of nature, and that the powers of nature are his servants (Psalm 104.1–4). At decisive points in the story of Israel as the people of God, extra-ordinary events in the world of nature abound. This is particularly so at the time of the Exodus from Egypt and the wandering through the wilderness to the promised land. The Exodus is preceded by the plagues in Egypt (Exodus 7.14–12.32), while at the heart of the Exodus deliverance is the miracle at the Red Sea (or Sea of Reeds), when the Israelites passed over the sea unscathed and their enemies were engulfed by the waters (Exodus 14). During the wilderness wanderings there are the miracles of the provision of the quails and of the manna (Exodus 16.13–21), as well as water from the rock at Massah and Meribah (Exodus 17.1–7; Numbers 20.2–13). Extra-ordinary happenings in the world of nature are to be found throughout the OT, but they are concentrated particularly in the traditions about the Exodus and the wilderness wanderings, and in the traditions about Elijah and Elisha (1 Kings 17–2 Kings 13).

It is not the intention of this section to discuss the historicity of these extra-ordinary happenings. For a treatment of the question see J. W. Rogerson, *The Supernatural in the Old Testament.*[4] Two points are considered here. The first is whether ancient Israelites were so ignorant of scientific causes that they attributed to God what we would explain in 'natural' terms. The second is whether they found it easier than ourselves to believe that extra-ordinary events happened.

It is often pointed out that there is no word in Hebrew corresponding to our word 'miracle', and that the Hebrew words translated as 'sign' or 'wonder' refer to both ordinary and extra-ordinary events. It is also pointed out that the Israelites had not formulated 'laws of nature' and that therefore they had no idea of a fixed order of nature in which extra-ordinary events were exceptions. On the face of it, there is a difference here between ourselves and the ancient Israelites. For us, reality is subject to 'laws', and extra-ordinary events 'break' these laws. We are suspicious of reports about events that break 'laws of nature', and we do not find it easy to believe in extra-ordinary events as special actions of God. Ancient Israelites, on the other hand, being ignorant of the scientific causes of many things, could easily accept accounts of extra-ordinary events, and could see in them the direct activity of God.

If this contrast between ourselves and ancient Israelites is correctly described, two conclusions might be drawn. The first is that the OT reports of extra-ordinary events as special actions of God are not to be trusted, because they derive from a people whose understanding of reality was pre-scientific. The second is that the Israelites had an advantage over us (if it is an advantage) in that they could perceive God at work in events more easily than we can.

In fact, it is probably easy to exaggerate the difference between ourselves and the ancient Israelites in this matter. There is no

67

doubt that Israelites did not know the scientific causes of events such as eclipses and rainbows, and that they would have found it easier than us to see these as special actions of God. On the other hand, they knew much about the regularities of life. They observed keenly the habits of birds and animals (Jeremiah 8.7), they knew about the special properties of plants and their products (2 Kings 20.7). They had developed a rudimentary technology of metals, as well as agricultural skills. They had certainly built up a stock of practical knowledge in terms of which they were aware for most of the time which happenings were normal and which were extra-ordinary.

This is clearly borne out by the requests for signs that we find in the OT. When Gideon asked (Judges 6.36–40) that the fleece left out overnight should be wet and the ground dry, and on the second occasion that the fleece should be dry and the ground wet, he, and subsequent readers and hearers of the tradition, knew perfectly well that something normally impossible was being requested. Although there is no Hebrew word for miracle, we would be well advised to accept that ancient Israelites were aware of what we call miracles. At the various crisis-points in Israel's history, the OT writers relate not normal, but extra-ordinary events, as they express their conviction that God had been acting for his people by expressing his lordship over nature.

Was it easier for ancient Israelites to 'see' God at work in the world than it is for us? The answer at one level is that in all societies, primitive, ancient or modern, there are to be found in similar proportions sceptics, those who will keep an open mind, and the gullible, who long for stories or experiences of the abnormal and who will believe almost anything. In our own society we know that there are people who are convinced that our planet is regularly visited by beings from other planets or from outer space. Although any generalization here is only a guess, we should reckon with the likelihood that some ancient Israelites would have found it harder to believe in miracles than some modern people, and that some ancient Israelites would have found it easier to believe in miracles than some modern people.

The OT informs us that there were those in Israel who said 'there is no God' (Psalm 14.1), while there were others who acted as though God had no interest in the affairs of the world (Psalm 73.11). There is also the fact that has been discussed earlier, that many ordinary people found other religions more helpful than that of the God of Israel. Whatever opinions we come to hold about the historicity of the miracles narrated in the OT, we should not conclude that faith in God in the OT was the product of a pre-scientific mentality that somehow made faith in God 'easy'.

## Sacrifice

Of all parts of the OT, those dealing with sacrifice seem to be the most foreign to us today. We have no experience of the whole business of regular killing, dissecting, blood-sprinkling, burning and disposal of the remains of animals and birds, and we find it difficult to imagine what it could have meant in ancient Israel. We may think that the material dealing with sacrifice is unimportant for at least two reasons. First, if we are Christians, we believe that the death of Jesus has abolished the need for a sacrificial system such as we find in the OT. Second, we may think that sacrifice does not belong to the heart of OT religion at its best.

In some of the prophetic books, it appears to be said that God does not want animal sacrifices (Isaiah 1.12–20; Jeremiah 7.21-6; Amos 5.32–4). Then there are 'spiritualization' passages, in which it appears to be said that sacrifices of praise, thanksgiving and penitence are preferable to animal sacrifices (Psalm 51.15–17; Micah 6.6–8). It may be attractive to think that the prophets and psalmists were radical before their time. The fact is that no reform movement from within the religion of the OT succeeded in abolishing the sacrificial system, for the simple reason that sacrifice was part of a much more complex system of drawing and maintaining boundaries in ancient Israel. Sacrifice cannot be extracted from the world-view of the OT without considerable damage to the whole fabric; and the sacrificial system was brought to an end only by major upheavals from outside. The first, when the temple was destroyed by the Babylonians in 587 BCE, ended sacrifices temporarily (although some scholars maintain that some sort of system continued until the rebuilding of the temple and the full restoration of sacrifice in 516 BCE). The second upheaval, when the Romans destroyed the temple in 70 CE, brought sacrifice permanently to an end. Sacrifice, then, was part of a system of behaviour that had such deep social roots that although it may have been subjected to violent criticism, only a major upheaval brought it to an end.

Sacrifice in the OT was a form of symbolic behaviour that enabled boundaries to be crossed, and boundaries to be restored when they had been violated. As stated earlier, the most fundamental boundary, so far as sacrifice was concerned, was that between clean and unclean. This cut right across the distinction that we make today between moral offences (the breaking of rules governing behaviour towards other human beings) and ritual offences (the breaking of rules about religious ceremonies, or about unclean objects). A person could become unclean, and thus violate the boundary between clean and unclean, in many ways: by contact with a dead body (Leviticus 22.4), or with an unclean animal (Lev. 11.24–7); by contracting 'leprosy' (Lev. 13–14), by menstruating or giving birth (Lev. 12.1–8; 15.19ff.), by damaging the property of another person (Lev. 6.1–7) or by breaking a divine commandment unintentionally (Lev. 5.14–19).

How sacrifice enabled boundaries to be crossed and restored is best illustrated by the ritual for rehabilitating the 'leper' in Lev. 14. On being declared a leper, a person was excluded from society. This was no doubt sound from the public health point of view. But at a deeper level, the exclusion came about because the leper had contracted a form of uncleanness and, as such, could not remain inside the boundaries that divided ordered social relationships from the disordered sphere beyond. The fact that the leper had to live outside the town or village indicates the way in which the land was also thought to be ordered into spheres reflecting order and chaos.

The ritual began with the priest meeting the leper 'outside the camp' (Lev. 14.3), that is, outside the sphere of ordered relationships. An elaborate ritual (including the release of a bird, which probably symbolized the removal of uncleanness) brought the leper into an intermediate state between society and outside of it. For seven days the leper lived inside the camp but outside his tent (Lev. 14.8). On the eighth day, a final elaborate ritual completed the passage back to full membership of society.

This ritual can be usefully compared with two other ceremonies. The first was that for consecrating priests in Lev. 8–9. What is common to the rituals is the seven days spent in an intermediate position. In the case of the priests, they are crossing the boundary between the ordinary and the sacred, and they spend seven days at the door of the tent of meeting, forbidden to enter the tent. They are thus part-way on their passage from the ordinary to the sacred, and they only finally enter the tent of meeting after the completion of their transition on the eighth day. The other ritual that can be compared is that for the Day of Atonement in Lev. 16. What is noteworthy here is the use of sacred space. The goat that is to bear the sins of the community is led through the camp, and out into the wilderness. Thus is symbolized the removal of uncleanness from the ordered to the chaotic, as represented by the wilderness.

This account of sacrifice, as well as concentrating upon ceremonies concerned with the removal of uncleanness and of crossing boundaries, not to mention many offerings that were designed simply to express thanks and gratitude to God, has described a view of reality that was not unique to the ancient Israelites. This view is to some extent common to all peoples who practise sacrifice. What was distinctive about OT sacrifice was the story in the context of which it was set. The whole system is presented in the OT as having been instituted by God on Mount Sinai after the Exodus. The fact that modern scholarship has shown that many elements of sacrifice were probably taken over from Israel's neighbours is not relevant here. As part of a coherent set of symbols, whatever the origin of some of those symbols, the sacrifices are given coherence and meaning by the Sinai story. The law-giving is presented in the OT as God's gift to his people after he had delivered them from slavery in Egypt. Sacrifices are thus part of the way in which Israel must respond in gratitude to God for his gracious redemption and his continuing care for the people. The sacrificial system enabled the Israelites to order their lives in loyalty to the God who had revealed himself at the Exodus. If and when they broke his laws, the sacrifices enabled relationships to be restored.

No mention has been made so far of such serious offences as murder, adultery and blasphemy, nor of the sacrifices prescribed in these cases. In fact, no sacrifices were prescribed for these and similar offences, because the death penalty was prescribed instead (e.g. Exodus 21.12–17). We do not know to what extent the death penalty was carried out in such cases. In the case of the family of David, David's adultery with Bathsheba was punished only indirectly (the child conceived by Bathsheba died), although he was strongly condemned and then forgiven in the name of God by the prophet Nathan. Absalom's murder of his brother seems to have gone unpunished, apart from banishment (cf. 2 Sam. 11–13 for all these events). If execution for serious offences was carried out regularly in ancient Israel, it is likely that, as in other societies, such executions involved rituals

71

designed to indicate that when society takes the life of an individual, this is no light matter. There is a sense in which such an execution is a sacrifice in which no animal can substitute for the criminal.[5]

It is clear from the OT that sacrifices were abused; that people thought that mere observance of ritual would bring prosperity (cf. Amos 4.4–5). Perhaps a reason for this was that addiction to rival forms of religion, which did not set their rituals in the context of the story of the Exodus salvation, dulled the willingness of the people to observe the moral requirements of the God of the Exodus. Perhaps people who abused sacrifices had no feeling for sacrifice as a form of symbolic behaviour preserving boundaries and pointing to God. However, we shall understand the sacrificial aspects of Israelite life if we concentrate not on the abuses, but upon the interrelationship that obtained in ancient Israel between sacrifice and the social and moral order.

## Social organization

That ancient Israelite society was organized differently from modern Western society quickly becomes apparent to any reader of the OT. The social term most frequently met is 'tribe', and it is fundamental to much OT literature that the Israelites were divided into twelve 'tribes'. However, the term is notoriously difficult to define. It can refer either to a particular territory or to a large descent group or both, and in the latter case there can be the apparent contradiction that a member of a tribe by descent lives outside the tribe considered as a territorial unit.

Elsewhere, I have defined a tribe provisionally as 'the largest social unit for mutual defence against other Israelite social units'.[6] The purpose of this definition is to highlight the fact that in ancient Israel a person's rights were defended by the group or groups to which she or he belonged. In a local dispute, a person's immediate family would defend her or him against another family. If the dispute were wider, the village would defend a person against another village, and so on up to the level of tribe. That tribes had disputes and battles with each other is indicated in the stories in the book of Judges (cf. chapters 12, 20 and 21). The next level above tribe would be the whole nation.

Although the social term most frequently met in the OT is tribe, ancient Israelites in practice were less concerned with their tribe and more concerned with their local villages and families. Most villages had only a few hundred inhabitants, and although these were broadly related to each other, families lived together, in so-called four-roomed houses, in basic nuclear groups of four to seven persons. This basic family unit is called *bet 'av* in Hebrew, meaning father's house, although even this social term had several meanings. In Gen. 24.38 Abraham tells his servant to travel to Mesopotamia to seek a wife for Isaac from among 'his father's house'. In this instance, *bet 'av* is clearly a descent group. However, in Gen. 50.8 *bet 'av* can refer only to the nuclear family of which Joseph is head, consisting of Joseph, his wife and two sons (Gen. 48.9). Whether or not these stories are historically true, they reflect social realities that would be familiar to Israelite readers or hearers of the stories.

Beginners in OT study need to be aware that there is much that we do not know about ancient Israel's social organization, and that some assertions that have been made in recent years run ahead of the evidence. Several warnings will thus be indicated in what follows.

One term that has gained considerable currency is 'segmentary society'. These were observed in African societies and described in a book entitled *Tribes without Rulers*,[7] among others places. The title of the book is important in suggesting an egalitarian type of social organization without any central authority; and it is precisely this aspect of the term that has been applied to Israelite social organization in the pre-monarchic period. Indeed, this period has been portrayed as a kind of golden age sociologically, before the establishment of monarchy subjected the Israelites to taxation, military service and forced labour. In fact, the notion of segmentary society is complex, and I have argued elsewhere that if there are features that segmentary societies have in common, those features are lacking in what the OT tells us about Israel's social organization.[8] To take two examples, segmentary societies apparently regard fratricide (the murder of a brother by his brother) as regrettable, but not a crime, and do not specify any right of the first-born son to inheritance. The OT certainly regards fratricide as a crime (Gen. 4.1–16) and strongly affirms the right of the first-born son to be the major inheritor of his father (Deut. 21.15–17).

Another area in which caution needs to be exercised is in thinking about the Israelite state and the manner of its administration. An important difference between a modern state and the Israelite state(s) is that the latter had boundaries rather than borders. Boundaries were marked by the presence of fortified settlements, and rulers were more concerned to mark out and defend their boundaries than to control the towns and villages within those boundaries. This means that an energetic king with a small but powerful army could extend his territory in the sense of establishing and maintaining settlements on the boundaries, without exercising much control over the territory as a whole. This fact has at least two implications. First, it may help us to understand the claims made in the Bible for the 'empire' of David and Solomon, which could have been staked out without in fact controlling territory outside the boundaries of Israel. Second, we may need to be cautious about supposing that, within Israel or Judah, the 'state' controlled the lives of ordinary villagers to any great extent. This is not to deny that unscrupulous kings or powerful landowners could harm villagers by making excessive demands upon them. It is to warn us that the misfortunes that afflicted families in villages could also result from conflicts within and between families at the local level.

This last observation leads on to a most important point. There is a tendency in recent political discussion in Britain and North America to idealize 'the family' and family values, and even to suppose that the Bible in some way supports this concern. In fact, the term family is as difficult to define as the term tribe, and even a moment's reflection upon 'traditional' families in today's society will indicate that there is the world of difference between aristocratic families that send their children to boarding schools for much of the year, middle-class families in which young children are cared for by child-minders while both parents go out to work, and families where the children do not go to school but are educated at home. To generalize about families and family values is precarious. Also, if one looks for help from the OT, the result is not reassuring: Cain kills his brother Abel (Gen. 4.26), Joseph's brothers sell him into slavery (Gen. 37.28), Abimelech has all his brothers killed (Judg. 9.1–6), Amnon rapes his half-sister Tamar and is then killed by his half-brother Absalom (2 Sam. 13.1–29).

In fact what is important in what the OT says about social relationships is the way in which it takes what ought *ideally* to be functions of family groups – supporting family members especially in times of difficulty – and extends these obligations to the whole people. This is seen in Deuteronomy 15.7–11, where the obligation of a family to support a member who has become poor becomes an obligation to *all* Israelites to support *any other Israelite* who has become poor.

Thus beginners in OT study need to be aware of the very different social conditions that existed in ancient Israel compared with their own society. But they also need to know that the OT was aware of the limitations of 'natural' social organization, and that it confronted ancient Israel with moral obligations that were based upon Israel's belief in God's graciousness, and the need to reflect that graciousness in the organization of daily life.

## NOTES

1 The sort of view that I have in mind is presented in the essay 'Myth and Reality', in H. Frankfort and others, *Before Philosophy* (Harmondsworth, Penguin, 1949); complete edn, *The Intellectual Adventure of Ancient Man* (Chicago, University of Chicago, 1946).

2 See further J. Rogerson, *Atlas of the Bible* (Oxford, Andromeda, 1985).

3 For a much fuller discussion see J.W. Rogerson, *Anthropology and the Old Testament* (Oxford, Blackwell, 1978; Atlanta, John Knox, 1979, reprint Sheffield, Sheffield Academic Press, 1984), pp. 47–51.

4 J.W. Rogerson, *The Supernatural in the Old Testament* (Guildford, Lutterworth, 1976); B. Kaye and J.W. Rogerson, *Miracles and Mysteries in the Bible* (Philadelphia, Westminster, 1978).

5 See M.F.C. Bourdillon in M. Fortes and M.F.C. Bourdillon (eds.), *Sacrifice* (London, Academic, 1980), p. 13. In the same volume see also the article by J.W. Rogerson, 'Sacrifice in the Old Testament: Problems of Method and Approach', pp. 45–59.

6 See J. Rogerson and P. Davies, *The Old Testament World* (Cambridge, CUP, 1989), p. 58.

7 J. Middleton and D. Tait (eds.), *Tribes without Rulers – Studies in African Segmentary Systems* (London, Routledge & Kegan Paul, 1958).

8 See J.W. Rogerson, 'Was Early Israel a Segmentary Society?' in *Journal for the Study of the Old Testament* 36 (1986), pp. 17–26.

## FURTHER READING

On genealogies: R.R. Wilson, *Genealogy and History in the Biblical World* (New Haven, Yale University, 1977).

On the world of nature and its division into spheres: Mary Douglas, *Purity and Danger* (London, Routledge, 1966); *Implicit Meanings – Essays in Anthropology* (London, Routledge, 1975), pp. 303–5. Also J.W. Rogerson, 'The Old Testament View of Nature: Some Preliminary Questions', in *Oudtestamentische Studiën*, XX (1977), pp. 67–84.

On sacrifice: the volume edited by Fortes and Bourdillon (note 5 above). On magic: Rogerson, *Anthropology* (see note 3 above).

Also, C.S. Rodd, 'The Family in the Old Testament', *The Bible Translator*, vol. 18 (1967), pp. 19–26. A good general introduction to social structure is R. Fox, *Kinship and Marriage* (Harmondsworth, Penguin, 1967).

# 5

## The Individual and the Community

### PAUL JOYCE

The reader of the Old Testament cannot help being struck by the importance attached in ancient Israel to the social group or community. The important unit when dealing with morality, law and religion in the OT often seems to be not so much the individual as the group to which he belongs. The Israelite looks to his family for aid and protection, particularly when his property or the continuation of his name are threatened. For example, when a man died and left a childless widow, the man's brother was expected to marry her, and the first son of this union was to succeed to the name of the dead brother, 'that his name may not be blotted out of Israel' (Deut. 25.6). Or again, if a poor man was forced to sell his property or even sell himself into slavery, a close relative was expected to act as *Goel* or Redeemer, and bail out the poor relative, so as to keep the property – or the man – in the family (Lev. 25.25, cf. vv. 39–43).

There could also be a negative side to this strong sense of community. In the case of a sin or a crime, the whole family of the man who actually committed the act could be punished, even though they had nothing to do with the offence. For example, in 2 Sam. 21, seven descendants of Saul are executed so as to remove the guilt incurred by their ancestor Saul when he put to death some Gibeonites. Or again, in Joshua 7, when Achan is executed for stealing some valuables that had been seized in battle but that had been dedicated to God, his entire family is executed with him.

In addition to his immediate family or household, the ancient Israelite usually regarded himself as belonging to an extended family. And then, more widely still, he regarded himself as belonging to one of the tribes of Israel. Finally and most importantly, the Israelite was strongly aware of being one of the 'Sons of Israel', the people of Yahweh, and it was above all from this sense of being part of a nation that the ancient Israelite seems to have derived his personal sense of identity.[1]

Yahweh was first and foremost the God of the people of Israel; one might say that he was only the God of the individual Israelite in so far as the individual participated in the nation of Israel, which regarded itself as chosen for a special relationship with Yahweh. Religious experience seems normally to be viewed in the OT in the broad setting of the community. It is not surprising, then, that this community of Israel sems to have relied above all on the worship of the one God, Yahweh, as the great uniting principle of its life. As Israel began to become more conscious of its unity as a nation, during the period from about 1200 to 1000 BCE, it seems to have been common allegiance to one God, rather than any highly organized political organization, that gave this mixed group of people a growing sense of shared identity.[2] And later, in the period after the Exile of Judah in Babylonia in the sixth century BCE, it seems to have been worship that was the essential bond uniting the people of Israel. (It is significant that the name Israel is still used in this later period to describe the worshipping people of Yahweh, even though the political entity known as Israel, the northern sister kingdom of southern Judah, had long since ceased to exist.) Israel after the Exile typically viewed itself as the holy people of Yahweh gathered around his sanctuary in Jerusalem. The boundaries of this community were made all the clearer by the emphasis placed on specifically Jewish practices such as circumcision and Sabbath observance. Those who in serious respects broke the sacred law of Moses, increasingly the focus of religious life, could be excommunicated, or expelled from the community, so as to preserve the purity of Israel as the holy people of Yahweh. Moreover, within this community of the people of Yahweh, we find worship as an essential uniting factor also for smaller groups in society. For example, the Passover was very much a family festival celebrated at home, and as such was one of the essential bonds of Israelite family life.

It may be said, then, that in ancient Israel the community, whether the immediate family, the extended family, the tribe or the nation itself, was of enormous importance, and that there was a close link between the worshipping life of Israel and this strong sense of community. It is true to say that many aspects of this strong sense of community, particularly those relating to the punishment of sin or crime noted earlier, strike the modern reader as somewhat strange, even at times immoral. However, it should not be thought that the tendency to think in terms of a community or a corporate group is entirely alien to our experience. For example, when speaking of a committee or a football team we often tend to imply that the group involved has a kind of personality of its own. We are aware of a tension in our thinking between the corporate group and the individuals of whom it is made up; and this tension is often reflected in the inconsistency of our language, referring to the committee, for example, at one moment as 'they' and, at the next, as 'it'. Or again, in contemporary worship, it is not unknown for the prayers of the congregation to be summed up in a prayer that uses the word 'I' in a sense meant to represent all those present.

Despite such modern parallels to much of what we find in the OT, some scholars have felt that the strong emphasis on the community in ancient Israel calls for further explanation. Some have even argued that it is to be seen as the result of a different psychology, an altogether different way of viewing the world. The best known advocate of such a theory was H. Wheeler Robinson,[3] who argued that in ancient Israel the limits of an individual's personality were not clearly defined and that much of the OT is to be understood in the light of the alleged fact that the individual was not even distinguished from the group to which he belonged. The group, said Robinson, could be thought of as having a 'Corporate Personality'. Thus, in the case of the story of Achan in Joshua 7, the guilt of the one man, Achan, extended to the group to which he belonged. At first, the whole people of Israel are defeated in battle, but later, when Achan is isolated as the culprit, his whole family is executed with him. This is appropriate, argued Robinson, because Achan's personality is thought of as extending into the group. In speaking of Corporate Personality in this way, Robinson was attempting to give a rather bold psychological explanation for cases such as that of Achan. He was arguing, in large part on the basis of some of the books on anthropology that appeared in the early part of this century, that ancient Israel's thinking in this area was really that of a primitive or pre-logical people, and that only when this was recognized could the OT be understood correctly. Robinson, and a number of scholars who were influenced by him, used this theory to try to explain a variety of puzzling features in the OT. For example, in the central section of the book of Isaiah, we find the figure of the Suffering Servant of Yahweh. Scholars have long discussed the meaning and significance of the passages that refer to the Servant. One problem is that sometimes the Servant is spoken of as Israel (e.g. Isa. 49.3) and at other times he sounds much more like an individual (especially in chapter 53). Robinson argued that the Servant was indeed sometimes viewed as a corporate group and at other times as an individual, but he went on to give an explanation of this based on his theory of Corporate Personality, claiming that the ancient Israelite mind was capable of a swift transition from the one to the many, and vice versa, an ability quite unparalleled in our modern way of thinking.[4] Another feature of the OT that has long puzzled scholars is the way that in many of the Psalms there is an inconsistency in the use of the singular and the plural. For example, in Psalm 44 we read in verse 4:

Thou art my King

and similarly in verse 6,

For not in my bow do I trust,

and yet in verse 5 we read,

Through thee we push down our foes

and again in verse 7,

Thou hast saved us from our foes.

Robinson felt that such inconsistency between 'I' and 'we' demanded some such psychological explanation as his theory of Corporate Personality. The Psalmist, he felt, really did not distinguish the individual from the group and so slid easily from one to the other.

We must ask ourselves, however, whether the evidence of the OT does indeed demand such an explanation. Scholars have suggested plausible alternative explanations for particular cases. For example, it has been suggested that the reason Achan's family is executed with him is not that his personality is thought of as extending into them in some way; rather that Achan's family are regarded as his property. Their destruction is part of Achan's punishment. Moreover, it has been persuasively argued that the anthropological studies upon which Robinson based his notion of Corporate Personality are now outdated and discredited.[5] There is, however, a still more basic criticism that can be made of his theory, namely that it seems to deny to the ancient Israelite the awareness of being an individual that the modern obviously has. Robinson does in fact speak of the OT as being produced 'prior to the development of the modern sense of personality', but it is by no means clear that it is appropriate or necessary to speak of ancient Israel as a 'primitive' people or of its thinking as 'pre-logical'. At no point does the emphasis on the community in the OT demand that the ancient Israelites should have had a psychology essentially different from our own. We have already suggested a number of modern examples (the committee or the football team) where we tend to attribute a kind of personality to a corporate group; but no one would suggest for a moment that this is because we are unable to distinguish between groups and individuals. Why, then, should we suppose that the ancient Israelites were unable to make such distinctions? We are quite familiar with the personification of nations – for example, the figure of Britannia – or of other groups, as in the memorials to the Unknown Soldier. When discussing history, politics or sociology, we inevitably become aware of the tension between speaking of corporate groups and social forces on the one hand and real individual human beings on the other. The complexities and tensions of the relationship between groups and the individuals of whom they are made up are an inescapable fact of human life in all ages. These are things we share in common with the ancient Israelites rather than things that set them apart from us. Certainly, cultures differ enormously one from another (this is one of the primary lessons of all historical study), and we do feel a sense of injustice at the fate of Achan's family, wishing to regard them as innocent individuals. But the differences are not to be exaggerated: the differences between cultures are rarely absolute, they are almost always differences of degree. It is fair to say that for the most part the OT does convey a stronger sense of the importance of the community and of corporate groups than we are used to, and this does give rise to what seem to us to be injustices and anomalies. But this does not mean that we should regard the OT as the literature of a primitive people, totally alien to modern western thinking.

We have dwelt on H. Wheeler Robinson's theory of Corporate Personality not only because of its direct importance for the question of the individual and the community in Israel, but also because it provides a salutary warning of the tendency of such scholarly notions to become taken for granted and employed somewhat indiscriminately in biblical studies. To begin with, the theory was advanced as a psychological explanation of certain perplexing passages such as that relating to Achan. Then, it came to be regarded by Robinson as an essential feature of 'Israelite Thought' as such, and soon it came to be applied by Robinson and many others to a host of passages and issues in the OT, and also the New Testament. The notion of Corporate Personality is occasionally vague and confusing even in Robinson's own writings,[6] but in the hands of others it was often used even more loosely. We shall see later that it is in any case always risky to speak about typical 'Israelite Thought' as something that may be precisely described (largely because Israel and its literature contain such an enormous variety of ways of thinking), but such language is even more suspect when it involves a notion as ill-founded as Robinson's Corporate Personality. The new student of biblical studies would do well to be aware that fashions are as common in scholarship as in any other area of life. A notion such as Corporate Personality can be like a band-wagon onto which numerous scholars jump, often ill-advisedly; and such ideas can equally quickly fall out of fashion. The student should learn to read the works of biblical scholars with a critical eye; he or she will often find different opinions being expressed and should soon acquire the ability to spot the particular axe an author has to grind. This should not be a cause of anxiety; it is part of what makes biblical studies such a rich and exciting field. Above all, students should have the courage to make up their own minds, and that is best done by balancing the reading of books about the Bible by careful reading of the biblical text itself.

Another very widely held notion about the OT, perhaps even more influential than Robinson's theory of Corporate Personality, is that which suggests that there was a steady, and trace-able, development in Israel's thinking away from a strong emphasis on the community (such as we have considered) towards an ever-increasing emphasis on the individual. This has long been, and remains, a prevalent view both in scholarly works on the OT and in more popular presentations.[7] However, the basis of this notion is by no means as sound as is commonly assumed. It will be useful for us to look at this question now, not only because this should shed further light on our topic of the individual and the community in Israel, but also because such an enquiry should again highlight various more general features of OT study.

The developmentalist view we are considering envisages a shift away from the strong emphasis on the community and corporate responsibility, of which the Achan case is often cited as an example, to a situation in which each individual Israelite is held responsible for his own deeds. It is usually suggested that the crucial stage in this development was the period of Judah's Exile in Babylonia in the sixth century BCE, with the words of the prophet Ezekiel usually being regarded as an especially important step in the development of individualism in Israelite thought. This long development is often seen as playing an important part in preparing the ground for the Christian revelation.

However, in attempting to create a neat system, this simple theory in fact misrepresents a much more complicated set of data. To begin with, an important distinction needs to be made between, on the one hand, language about criminal law on the human level and, on the other hand, language about God's punishment of human sin. In criminal law, a crime is committed and eventually, when the culprit has been detained and found guilty, the appropriate punishment is imposed. In Deuteronomy 24.16, in a legal passage, we read, 'The fathers shall not be put to death for the children, nor shall the children be put to death for the fathers; every man shall be put to death for his own sin.' In its present form, this verse probably comes from the seventh century BCE, but most scholars concede that, in the area of Israel's criminal law, the general principle from the earliest times seems to have been that justice demanded that the individual responsible for a crime should be isolated and punished. The situation is rather different, however, when we turn to consider language about God's punishment of human sin. It is here that we find the strongest tendency to think in terms of whole groups of people being responsible and being punished; and the reason is not difficult to see. Ideas about God punishing human sin tend to start from an experience of hardship or suffering that calls for explanation. A common explanation for hardship in ancient Israel, as in many other cultures, was that God must be angry and must be punishing wrongdoing. However, in these circumstances it was often difficult to identify the particular wrong in question, and so the tendency was to think in general terms of the group or of all Israel as a people having displeased God. Moreover, where even this did not seem to offer a satisfactory explanation for the hardships being suffered, a longer-term view could be taken. One could explain present suffering that was apparently undeserved by looking back in history to some notorious sin that could be seen as the cause of God's wrath. Thus, for example, when the authors of the Books of Kings (see 2 Kings 23.26–7) attempted to account for the great disaster of 587 BCE, when Babylonia destroyed the Jerusalem temple and exiled many Judeans, they looked back to the notorious sins of Manasseh, who had been King of Judah in the seventh century BCE. And so it is that we find the idea of inherited guilt; Israel is thought of as a community extending through history, and the generation alive in 587 BCE can be thought of as being punished for sins that, strictly speaking, they did not commit. We must remember, then, that when we ask questions about how responsibility was understood in Israel, the situation is likely to vary according to the area of responsibility being discussed, and that the stronger emphasis on group responsibility is likely to be found mainly in the area of language about God's punishment of sin.

However, the even more basic point to grasp is that it seems that throughout Israel's history, we find both communal and more individualistic elements in language about responsibility. Even in the area of language about God's punishment of sin we find at an early date some feeling that it was somehow unsatisfactory to envisage Yahweh acting in history in a way less fair than the normal practice of Israel's criminal law, where the general principle at least was that the guilty man should be the one to be punished. So, for example, in Genesis 18, possibly written as early as the tenth century BCE,[8] Abraham pleads with Yahweh not to punish the righteous people of Sodom along with the wicked. In verse 25, we read:

> Far be it from thee . . . to slay the righteous with the wicked . . .
> Shall not the judge of all the earth do right?

Moreover, just as we find here, early in Israel's history, a concern for the fair treatment of the righteous individual, we also find in the very late period of OT times a certain amount of material envisaging those who, strictly speaking, are innocent being included in the punishment of the guilty. For example, in Daniel 6.24, when Daniel's wicked accusers are cast into the den of lions, the same fate befalls their children and their wives. Even in the NT we find some examples of the notion of inherited guilt mentioned earlier. In Matthew 23.35, Jesus is portrayed as foretelling that upon the scribes and Pharisees of his own day will come

> all the righteous blood shed on earth, from the blood of innocent Abel to the blood of Zechariah the son of Barachiah.

The simple developmental theory that pictures a steady growth in Israelite thought from communal responsibility to individual responsibility does not do justice to such evidence.

Even within a single passage in the OT we often find a complex combination of communal and individualistic elements. For example, in the story of Achan in Joshua 7, at first all Israel suffers defeat in battle because of Achan's sin, which suggests a strong emphasis on Israel as a group. Joshua then sets about discovering the guilty person, clearly a much more individualistic concern; and yet when Achan is isolated and punished, all his family are executed along with him. Genesis 18 provides another example of such complexity. We have seen that Abraham pleads with Yahweh not to include righteous individuals in the general destruction of Sodom; and yet the solution proposed is that if ten righteous be found, the whole city should be spared, an idea that seems to reflect a tendency to think in terms of the community as the really important unit. These two passages, then, each seem to combine a variety of ways of viewing responsibility. They also illustrate another important point. So much of the evidence with which we have to deal in the OT is in story form. Such stories were not intended to present a systematic theology, and though they are of help to us in our study of ideas and beliefs held in Israel, we would be very foolish to try to extract from such materials an overall Israelite theology of responsibility.

As was mentioned earlier, the work of the prophet Ezekiel has often been taken to represent a particularly important stage in the alleged steady development from a communal to an individualistic emphasis in Israel's thinking about responsibility. Ezekiel has been regarded as the great prophet of individualism, his teaching in the first half of the sixth century marking the crucial turning point away from the old ideas of corporate

85

responsibility and towards the supposedly new truth of individual responsibility. However, this is a misrepresentation. As we have seen, there were important elements of individualism in thought about responsibility in Israel from an early date, certainly earlier than Ezekiel's work in the sixth century BCE. It is, moreover, in any case by no means clear that Ezekiel was concerned to stress individual responsibility. Chapter 18 of his book is the one most often cited by those who would claim that individualism is a prominent feature of Ezekiel's teaching. An examination, albeit brief, of that chapter will provide an illustration of the necessity, when considering issues like this, to ask especially carefully what a particular chapter is saying.

A careful reading of chapter 18 of Ezekiel reveals that Ezekiel's purpose is not to argue that particular individuals will be judged in isolation from their contemporaries. His concern is not with individuals at all. Rather, he addresses the house of Israel in a national crisis, the subjugation of Judah by Babylonia and the exile of many of her people. This catastrophe inevitably affected the whole nation, and so it is the house of Israel as a community that Ezekiel addresses. He says they are no longer to blame the sins of their ancestors for the present situation. They are not to use the proverb, 'The fathers have eaten sour grapes and the children's teeth are set on edge' (vv. 2–3). Here Ezekiel criticizes the idea of inherited guilt we mentioned earlier; the present generation must, he says, accept responsibility for its own situation. It is very important to note (the point is often missed) that in rejecting the idea of inherited guilt, Ezekiel does not attempt to put in its place a theory of individual responsibility. Rather, he calls on the present generation to stop blaming past generations and, as the community of the house of Israel alive today, to turn to Yahweh.

To illustrate his point, Ezekiel pictures three men: a righteous man, his wicked son and his righteous grandson (Ezekiel 18.5–18). Ezekiel appeals (in v. 20) to the general principle, which, as we have said, seems to have been the working basis of Israel's criminal law from early times, namely that it is the guilty man who should be punished. Accordingly, it is said that the righteous man shall live and that the wicked son shall die, despite his father's righteousness. Then we come to the really crucial case. Ezekiel says that the righteous grandson shall live; he shall not die for his father's sins. It is vital to note that Ezekiel is here giving an illustration of the situation of the nation Israel in its present crisis in history. His point is that the present generation suffering conquest and exile must be suffering for their own sins; if they were righteous they would not be suffering. It is easy enough to see how this section of chapter 18, picturing the three men, could be misread as an argument for individual responsibility. Certainly, it takes for granted and appeals to the general principle of individual responsibility as normally applied in criminal law (i.e. it is the guilty man who should be punished), but when we read this section of the chapter in the context of the chapter as a whole it becomes clear that Ezekiel is addressing a given historical situation and answering the question why the nation is suffering as it is.

Ezekiel's purpose in all this is very positive: he wishes to persuade his audience of their responsibility so that he can challenge them to repent. In the section beginning at verse 21, he stresses that if a wicked man repents, his past will be forgotten, and that if a righteous man falls into sin, he will not be spared punishment on account of his previous righteousness. Again, all this relates to the situation of the nation Israel, Ezekiel's point being that if the community, acknowledging its responsibility and its sin, repents, it will not be punished for its previous sins. The present generation of Israel is not only free of the punitive effects of the sins of past generations; but more, the community may even become free of the punitive effects of its own past sins. The whole argument of chapter 18 is presented very subtly by Ezekiel to lead his audience into a position where they may respond to his very positive challenge to 'turn and live'.[9] We know from Ezekiel 9 that the prophet was not altogether unconcerned about the fact that some innocent people might suffer in the present crisis, but for the most part he really does not concern himself with this problem, because his primary task is to address and explain a given disaster affecting the nation as a whole, a disaster he can even describe, in a rhetorical phrase, as cutting off 'both righteous and wicked' (Ezekiel 21.3). This is a strange phrase indeed to find in a book so often seen as representing the crucial state in the alleged development in Israel's thought from corporate responsibility to individual responsibility. Surely this way of viewing Ezekiel seriously misrepresents the biblical evidence.

Let us accept, though, that some OT material does suggest that one trend in the complex area of thought about responsibility was towards a greater concern for the life of the individual. For example, the book of Job explores the problem of undeserved suffering and seems acutely aware of the enigma of a righteous individual living a life of anguish and distress. The book of Job is usually dated to the late period of the OT, after the Exile of Judah in Babylonia in the sixth century BCE. The same late period saw the development of the belief in personal resurrection, and it is likely that one influence on the growth of this belief was a sense that the lives of particular individuals should at some point receive appropriate reward (or sometimes punishment). Nevertheless, this concern with the individual is just part of the picture in post-exilic Israel, a complex picture that, as we have seen, contained a number of elements that viewed responsibility in more corporate and communal ways. We certainly cannot think of a simple one-way development towards individualism. Sometimes we may even detect shifts in the opposite direction. For example, some scholars have suggested that part of the originality of the great eighth-century prophet Amos was that, unlike some of his predecessors who had condemned particular individuals, he addressed a message of judgement to the nation of Israel as a whole. One further reason why we should be wary of the developmental theory we have been considering is the problem of the difficulty of dating material – an important issue in all biblical studies. Even if passages giving a straightforward line on responsibility were found (we have seen that complexity is more typical), they would have to be datable to some degree of certainty if they were to lend support to a developmental theory. Such certainty is in fact rarely attainable.

We conclude, then, that the developmental theory relating to ideas about responsibility in Israel should be regarded with great caution, and we suggest that throughout Israel's history the complexities of the relationship between the individual and the group were for the most part recognized as clearly as they are today. The rich variety and complexity of the OT does not lend itself to neat patterns imposed upon it by scholars, and as a general rule one should always be suspicious of such systematizing.

More than once in this discussion we have warned against bold assertions about 'Israelite Thought', and it is appropriate now to look more directly at the question of unity and diversity in Israel, as a theme closely related to the issue of the individual and the community, the one and the many. It is risky to attempt to speak about Israelite Thought, either as a distinctive way of thinking or as a set list of beliefs, above all because there was in Israel such a wide variety of ways of thinking and such a broad range of beliefs. Indeed, there is a growing body of archaeological and other evidence to suggest that this range was even broader than the OT indicates. In this respect of diversity, ancient Israel was like any other culture. To be sure, as we saw at the start of this chapter, there was a particularly strong sense of national identity in Israel, based primarily not on ethnic or political identity, but rather on shared allegiance to the one God, Yahweh. Perhaps it was the very strength of this religious bond, sometimes described in terms of a covenant, or agreement, between Yahweh and Israel, that allowed there to be, within the broad unity of Israel, such a rich diversity of thought and belief. If we are to appreciate the full richness of this diversity, we should resist the tendency to think of the OT as one book, and view it rather as the library of a nation, reflecting that nation's varied experiences of God over many generations.[10]

It seems that the people who made up the nation of Israel really became conscious of themselves as forming a distinct nation during what we call the period of the Judges (from about 1200 to 1000 BCE). Many scholars believe that the traditions in the OT that speak about the period before that, the traditions of Abraham, Isaac and Jacob, and even perhaps the tradition of the Exodus from Egypt, may well all reflect the experiences of only parts of what later became Israel. It is likely that as the nation of Israel took shape during the period of the Judges, different groups (such as particular tribes) contributed stories about their own past histories to the national pool of tradition, and that when the first history of Israel's past came to be written (possibly as early as the tenth century BCE), these different elements were woven into the story of what was now regarded as the one nation, Israel, bound together by the worship of one God, Yahweh, whose hand was seen in all the many partial histories that now made up Israel's national history.[11]

However, even after the early period, basic differences remained between the parts making up the people of Israel. The most profound of these differences was that between North and South. In about 922 BCE, these two areas, which had formed a united monarchy under David and his son Solomon, fell apart when the northern territory broke away and established an independent monarchy. These two Hebrew kingdoms even fought wars with each other, and were in many respects very different from one another; certainly as different as, for example, England and Scotland. Many scholars attempt to trace certain parts of the literature of the OT to one or other of the Hebrew kingdoms. For example, many posit an early historical work usually called the Yahwist Work (and discerned within Genesis, Exodus and Numbers); it is commonly thought to derive from the South. On the other hand, most scholars trace the tradition represented in the book of Deuteronomy to the North. A confusing fact to be aware of is that the Northern Kingdom called itself Israel, in contrast to the Southern Kingdom which called itself Judah. Confusion can arise because the name Israel was also often used to describe the whole People of Yahweh (Northern and Southern), regardless of political divisions. The two kingdoms existed side by side until 721 BCE, when the empire of Assyria engulfed the North, exiling many of its inhabitants. A similar fate befell the South in 587 BCE, when the Jerusalem temple was destroyed by Babylon and many southerners were exiled to Babylonia. This created two communities of Judeans: those in Judah and those in Babylonia. Scholars attempt to assign the literature of this exilic period to one of these two communities. For example, the central section of Isaiah, chapters 40–55, often called the work of Second Isaiah, is usually thought to have been composed, for the most part at least, in exile in Babylonia, whereas the Book of Lamentations is usually regarded as deriving from exilic Judah. Such literature is generally seen to reflect the life and concerns of the particular community that produced it, but it must be admitted that it is often very difficult to be at all sure of the place of origin of the literature. Though some exiles returned from Babylonia later, many remained; and from this time onwards the widespread geographical diversity of the people of Yahweh further complicates the picture – we speak of the Dispersion of the Jewish people, Egypt being another place to which considerable numbers of Judeans moved, especially from the sixth century onwards (see Jer. 43.4–7). The northerners who were exiled by the Assyrians in 721 BCE disappear from view, but we catch occasional glimpses of the remnant of the northern community (e.g. in 2 Chron. 30). Later, we become aware of the existence in the North of the Samaritans, who were increasingly despised by the southern community, which regarded itself as the one true Israel.

In terms of geography alone, then, it may be seen that what we call Israel was an incredibly diverse phenomenon. Moreover, the time-scale covered by the OT is vast. It is really a library produced over a period of about a thousand years. Small wonder that the OT contains such a rich diversity of theology. For example, we find a number of different attitudes to the institution of the monarchy. If one reads 2 Samuel 7 or some of the so-called royal Psalms, such as Psalms 2 and 110, the Davidic monarchy is seen as a primary channel of Yahweh's favour to Israel. However, if one turns to 1 Samuel 8 or 12, or to Deuteronomy 17, monarchy seems to be seen as a rather dangerous threat to the true worship of Yahweh. Another example is provided by Israel's system of sacrificial worship. Large sections of the book of Leviticus, for example, are devoted to detailed legislation for this, but if one turns to the prophets, such as Isaiah or, more especially, Amos, one finds a vigorous criticism of Israel's complacent reliance on its system of sacrificial worship, which at times seems to come very close to an outright rejection of the whole system. And so within a community strongly conscious of itself as the one people of Yahweh, we nevertheless find a vast range of theological opinion and religious belief and an equally extensive range of ways of expressing these.

Recent years have seen much fruitful application of the insights and methods of sociology within OT study. This has further enriched our sense of the complexity of the social reality of ancient Israel.[12] The OT is the rich deposit of the lively theological tradition of this very diverse nation over many centuries; and it is this that makes it such an exciting subject of study.

To summarize, we began this chapter by considering the strong emphasis on the importance of the community that characterizes much of the OT. We noted, however, that we today sometimes think in terms of corporate groups as well as in terms of individuals, and we argued that it is therefore unreasonable to regard such language as reflecting a 'primitive' mentality when it is found in the OT. Next, we considered the theory that Israelite thought developed smoothly from an emphasis on the corporate responsibility of groups and communities towards an ever-increasing emphasis on the responsibility of the individual. We argued that this theory does not do justice to the evidence of the OT, which suggests rather that at all periods there were some corporate elements and some more individualistic elements in thought about responsibility in Israel. In the final section of the chapter, we suggested that it is, moreover, impossible to speak of 'Israelite Thought' as something that can be pinned down or described precisely, because Israel was such a diverse entity, extending through many centuries, increasingly spread out in many lands, and producing a great variety of religious literature. We noted the paradox that this rich diversity existed within a nation so strongly conscious of its identity as a community. This tension between diversity and unity may be said to reflect the tension between the individual and the community that we have seen to characterize the Old Testament as a whole. These are tensions that remain very much a part of our modern experience.

## NOTES

1 For fuller discussion of kinship and social organization, see Chapter 4. See also John Rogerson and Philip Davies, *The Old Testament World* (Cambridge, Cambridge University Press, 1989), Chapter 2, 'Social Organization'.

2 The process through which Israel had emerged as a nation has been the subject of keen debate over recent decades – see Chapter 3. See also George W. Ramsey, *The Quest for the Historical Israel: Reconstructing Israel's Early History* (London, SCM, 1982).

3 H.W. Robinson, *The Christian Doctrine of Man* (3rd edn, Edinburgh, T. & T. Clark, 1926). See especially Robinson's *Corporate Personality in Ancient Israel* (rev. edn, Philadelphia, Fortress, 1980; Edinburgh, T. & T. Clark, 1981).

4 H.W. Robinson, *The Cross in the Old Testament* (London, SCM, 1955), p. 77.

5 J.W. Rogerson, 'The Hebrew Conception of Corporate Personality', *Journal of Theological Studies* 21 (1970), pp. 1–16.

6 See Rogerson, *Journal of Theological Studies* 21 (1970).

7 For a classical presentation of this position see W. Eichrodt, *Theology of the Old Testament*, vol. ii (London, SCM, 1967; Philadelphia, Westminster, 1967), pp. 231–267.

8 It should be noted that most scholars are today much less confident than they once were about the dating of the material in the Pentateuch (Genesis–Deuteronomy). See Joseph Blenkinsopp, *The Pentateuch: An Introduction to the First Five Books of the Bible* (London, SCM, 1992), pp. 19–30.

9 Precisely how the call to repentance functions in Ezekiel is an interesting question. See further: Paul Joyce, *Divine Initiative and Human Response in Ezekiel* (Sheffield, JSOT Press, 1989), pp. 55–59. That book may also be consulted for a detailed exegesis of Ezekiel 18 (pp. 35–55) and a survey of ideas of collective and individual responsibility in the OT (pp. 779–87).

10 Such an approach, highlighting the diversity of the OT, can be very instructive. This is not, of course, to deny the importance of other modes of reading. For example, when the OT functions theologically as a scriptural canon, believers legitimately seek ways of reading it coherently as a whole. See also Chapter 6.

11  For a rather different, and more radical, approach to these questions, see Philip R. Davies, *In Search of 'Ancient Israel'* (Sheffield, JSOT Press, 1992).

12  See A.D.H. Mayes, *The Old Testament in Sociological Perspective* (London, Marshall Pickering, 1989).

## FURTHER READING

G.E. Mendenhall, 'The Relation of the Individual to Political Society in Ancient Israel', in J.M. Myers et al., ed., *Biblical Studies in Memory of H.C. Alleman* (Locust Valley, J.J. Augustin, 1960), pp. 89–108.

J.R. Porter, 'Legal Aspects of Corporate Personality', *Vetus Testamentum* 15 (1965), pp. 361–80.

# 6

## Old Testament Theology

### JOHN BARTON

I

Most Christians probably read the Old Testament to learn about God. They expect it to tell them what God is like, what he has done and what he requires of them. But those who approach the OT in this way are soon disappointed. They find that the God it shows them is, at best, something of a mixed blessing. Although at times he is loving, gentle and trustworthy, at others he seems capricious, harsh and unfeeling. The things he is said to have done include not only bestowing miraculous blessings (chiefly on the people of Israel), but also destroying whole nations without pity; and the conduct he demands, though it puts a high value on justice, often seems to lack compassion. The information about God we get from the OT seems fairly ambiguous, and we would be hard put to it to recognize in it the God in whom Jews or Christians now believe.

In one way the critical study of the OT described in the previous chapters alleviates the discomfort. A critical approach shifts the emphasis away from reading the OT to discover what God is like, and on to studying it in order to discover what the ancient Israelites *thought* he was like. Instead of learning what God has done, we learn what the authors or the communities who produced the various OT books *believed* he had done; and by applying historical methods we can sometimes discover what the actual events were that they interpreted as 'acts of God'. Rather than extracting from the Bible a catalogue of moral duties, we try to understand how ideas about ethics developed in ancient Israel. Because this puts us at one remove from the assertions the text itself makes about God, the problem of the more 'scandalous' parts of the OT becomes that much less acute. We are not being asked to say that God actually did or said or commanded what the OT says he did; only that people thought he had done so. OT study becomes the study of the history of Israelite religion, social life, and institutions. Since this makes no direct claims on our own religious allegiance, we can be much calmer and cooler about it than we could if we thought the OT was a source of direct information about God that had to be believed by religious people, just as it stood.[1]

But the loss here may be as great as the gain. In gaining an objective knowledge of religious beliefs in Israel, we seem to lose the Bible as a book of faith. The OT ceases to be a problem by becoming, from the believer's point of view, an irrelevance. The history of the religious beliefs of the ancient Israelites is an interesting subject for scholars to study, but it is not clear why students of theology – still less ordinary believers – should concern themselves with the OT, if this is all it can inform them about. If the OT is to continue to be important for theology, its usefulness will need to go beyond what merely historical study can offer. It is the attempt to provide this that is usually described as Old Testament Theology.

## II

One possibility for reuniting the OT with Christian theology may be called the 'winding quest' approach.[2] This says that the OT does not give us direct information about God; but by showing us the various stages through which the religious awareness of the Israelite people passed, it enables us to see how they were prepared for the fuller 'revelation' of God brought by Jesus. The OT is the record of various attempts to understand God, which were all more or less imperfect but which none the less were necessary steps on the path that eventually led to Christianity and the theology of the New Testament.

Thus the 'religious quest' of ancient Israel can be seen as a *gradual progress* towards the truth. The blood-thirsty religion and morality of the book of Judges, for example, represents an early stage of religious awareness that was gradually left behind as higher insights into God's nature made themselves known through the teaching of the prophets. The four-source hypothesis of the Pentateuch can be fitted well into such a theory of progressive revelation. The sources (J, E, D and P) derive from distinct phases within the history of ancient Israel, characterized by different types of religious thought, with J (the earliest source) reflecting an early and anthropomorphic idea of God, and P (the latest) a much more refined, transcendental and monotheistic faith.

So the OT bears witness to an enormous variety of religious insights and convictions, many of which strike us as crude or unacceptable but which were all necessary in paving the way for the pure monotheism that lies at the root of both Judaism and Christianity.[3] Without the warlike spirit exemplified in Judges, people would never have come to a serious awareness of the holiness of God, nor of his total and exclusive commands – however wrong they may have been to think that these demands meant destroying those who worshipped other gods. Without the ritualistic religion of temple and sacrifice, we should never have come to see the costliness of religious allegiance. And without the prophets, interpreting all the events of history as God's judgement or as his blessing, we should never have arrived at the belief that one God controls the entire course of the world according to principles of justice and mercy. All these types of OT religion were more or less flawed, but they represent essential stages through which human religious awareness had to pass if it was to lead, in the end, to the religious faith of modern believers.

A number of objections can be raised to this, even on the historical level. Against the idea of progressive revelation it can be pointed out that many of the ideas of early Israel were by no means dead in NT times. For example, the ideal of Holy War as set out in Joshua had enjoyed a resurgence in the second century BCE, in the days of the Maccabees. Christians have often thought that Judaism after the Exile regressed rather than made progress. Where the pre-exilic prophets had denounced Israel and threatened that God would destroy his own people for their sin, post-exilic prophecy and apocalyptic writing often confirmed the nation in its nationalism and were smugly complacent about God's grace towards it. We have seen that the four-source theory can be fitted into a framework of progressive revelation; but Wellhausen, who gave this theory its classic expression, did not at all see it in this way: he thought that P marked a decline into the narrow legalism and ritualism that would be condemned by Jesus and St Paul.

Even on the winding quest view, there are byways of OT faith and practice that cannot easily be seen as *necessary* preconditions of Judaism or Christianity. But there is also a more fundamental problem. If we are now at the end and goal of the quest, why should we concern ourselves so much with its earlier stages? If Israel's religious quest leads up to and is fulfilled in the religious systems of Christianity or Judaism, would we not do better to concentrate on the fulfilment, rather than to spend time on what it was a fulfilment of? Even if the OT is mainly of value as showing us how we got to where we are now, it is not clear that this answers the question why anyone concerned with religious *truth* in the present should still be interested in it. And this is a crucial question; for after all, it is the OT itself that is part of the Bible, not the reconstructions of stages in the religious awareness of ancient Israel that we can make from it. And it is presumably therefore the OT, not the reconstructions, that should be important to the modern believer.

## III

So 'OT theology' will have to be distinguished rather more sharply than this from the 'history of Israelite religious thought' if it is to be useful to us today. Perhaps a hopeful place to start is by noticing a feature we can easily fail to see when we are engaged on detailed, piecemeal study of the texts – a case of not seeing the wood for the trees. This feature is the obvious *family likeness* among the many different texts that make up the OT. Admittedly, the OT does not have the inner coherence of a collection of works by a single author, and there are a few books in it that strike even a casual reader as swimming against the current, or even as contradicting much that is said elsewhere – Ecclesiastes is the most obvious case. But we have only to try to imagine how the OT would strike someone brought up in a Far Eastern religious system, such as Hinduism or Taoism, or even a modern secular humanist, to realize that it is unmistakably the product of a single religious tradition with characteristic insights and emphases. The very fact that we feel Ecclesiastes is swimming against the current is a sign that there *is* a current, and that we have some idea of the direction it flows in.

Thus those who adopt the winding quest approach are clearly right in thinking that there is a certain unity in the religious thought of ancient Israel, even if what they build on this idea is less convincing. The OT may not be one book, but it is more than a random collection of 'texts from the world's great religions'. The texts composing it hang together with some coherence. And if we try to reconstruct the religious milieu these texts came from, we shall find that it looks like a reasonably unified religious culture. The books of the OT obviously do not come from a series of unrelated cultures that practised completely different religions. At one level, and for some purposes, we shall want to insist that all OT books are different – just as all English people are different, so that sweeping generalizations about an 'English mentality' are a travesty. But taking a longer view, it does make sense to talk of 'OT religion', just as it makes sense to generalize about 'the English' if we want to compare them with the Americans or the Japanese.

Beneath the assertions OT books make about what God is like, what he has done or what he has commanded – which vary a good deal – there are in fact a number of shared assumptions. The family likeness among OT texts owes as much to what is taken for granted as to what is positively asserted. One of the ways in which a system of belief can be identified is by noticing the points on which its adherents agree even when they are engaged in debate or disagreement with each other. Thus even when the prophets stress that God intervenes actively in human affairs (e.g. Amos 8.9–10), while Ecclesiastes denies that he does (e.g. Eccles. 1.9), they are working with the shared assumption that God is a being distinct from the world and transcending it, of whom it would at least make sense to say that he had or had not intervened. They are both equally far from a system such as pantheism, in which God simply *is* the world. In such a system, God cannot 'intervene' because he is not distinct from the world in the first place; to say he had intervened would be simply meaningless.

So instead of valuing some parts of the OT more highly than others, or following the development of Israelite thought reconstructed as lying behind it (as the winding quest approach does), we might try to identify its distinctive or characteristic features. This means looking for beliefs held in Israel, and attested in the OT, that can explain the family likeness shared by so much of this material.

## IV

Most modern approaches to OT theology have begun from approximately the point of view just outlined. They have rejected the simple distinction between the OT as a text (just as it stands) and the history of Israelite religious belief (as reconstructed by critical study of the OT). Instead, they have seen the two as inextricably bound up together. It would, indeed, be strange if the family likeness these books exhibit rested on a quite different basis from the family likeness that characterized the religion of the ancient Israelites; the study of the two things has to march in step. But identifying the basic features that make up the likeness is no easy task. One can often sense the distinctive atmosphere of a body of literature or of an historical period, but it is hard to analyse and describe this in a way that will satisfy others – even though they, too, may be convinced that there is indeed something distinctive about it. We shall consider the two most influential attempts at writing a 'Theology of the Old Testament' in the twentieth century, those of Walter Eichrodt[4] and Gerhard von Rad,[5] and then go on to examine the contribution made by the Biblical Theology Movement, whose influence is still important in many (especially popular) presentations of the subject, before going on to look at more recent developments.

Eichrodt published his *Theology of the Old Testament* over the years from 1933 to 1939; von Rad's *Old Testament Theology* appeared much more recently, in 1957–60. But they are alike in concentrating on what we have called the family likeness of the OT texts, at the level of what their writers explicitly said about God and Israel and the world. Eichrodt and von Rad both set out to present the faith of Israel, the body of beliefs that all who claimed to belong to the people of God in OT times were committed to (even though it changed and developed to some extent over time). This faith united the people of Israel, and it also united all or most of the writers of the OT, who were part of that people.

Both these scholars organized their presentation of the faith of Israel by taking one particular theme as the clue to the likeness among the majority of OT books. In Eichrodt's work the organizing principle is the covenant between God and Israel. The Israelites believed in a covenant-God, that is, a God who had chosen them from among all the nations and entered into a binding agreement with them that had the character of a contract, God promised to keep his side of the bargain, to continue the blessings he had begun in his act of choice – a choice Israel owed purely to his grace, and had done nothing to deserve. Israel, for its part, was under an obligation to maintain the contract by loyalty to God, exclusive worship of him, and obedience to his commands. These commands were summarized in law-codes (especially short digests such as the Ten Commandments), and also communicated from time to time through accredited prophets. It is the basic covenant-pattern that explains the common flavour of large tracts of the OT, and it was the Israelites' shared allegiance to the God of the covenant that kept the tribes united through their long history, and enabled them (alone among the nations of the ancient Near East) to live on as a religious community even after their national independence had been lost.

Von Rad's organizing principle is the saving history (or salvation history – *Heilsgeschichte*). For him, the distinctive and characteristic feature of the OT is a conviction that God directs the history of his people. He acts on their behalf, in accordance with a pattern of saving action first established when he led their ancestors out of their slavery in Egypt and gave them the Promised Land as their home. Passages such as Deut. 26.5–9, which von Rad believed to be very ancient, sum up the essential events that are the key to the way Israel's God acts. It was because they allowed this pattern to interpret all their experience that the Israelites were able to give coherence and meaning to the varied events that befell them in their long history. The same pattern provides the basic shape of the crucial first six books of the Bible, Genesis–Joshua (often called the Hexateuch). All the historical accounts of ancient Israel have the shape of the saving history: they are the record of God's acts with and for his people, guiding them and delivering them from their enemies.

It is important to see that in the work of these two scholars, and indeed in most OT theologies, we are not being asked to believe that the OT speaks with a single and unambiguous voice. A theology of the OT, as Eichrodt and von Rad understood it, is about the main stream of faith in Israel; and in a work as large as the OT, any attempt to identify this main stream is likely to run into a certain number of exceptions. But so long as the great bulk of the OT material seems to make sense when read from this point of view, the attempt is broadly justified. Both Eichrodt's and von Rad's theologies – still the most important theologies so far produced – do enable readers to find their way through the OT and to feel its characteristic atmosphere. Although they repay detailed study, both also lend themselves to being read fairly quickly so as to pick up the main thread of what is being said. Both, in different ways, present a picture of ancient Israel's faith that owes a lot to the book of Deuteronomy; and a good way to start work on the theology of the OT is to read Deuteronomy, perhaps with a straightforward commentary,[6] in conjunction with either Eichrodt or von Rad.

But do such statements of the theology of the OT help us find a use for the OT within theology? They still seem to be essentially historical statements about the beliefs of ancient Israelites, even if they are at a higher level of generality and sophistication than piecemeal studies of the theology of this or that biblical writer. But Eichrodt and von Rad both claimed that their work constituted 'theology' in a more profound sense than this. They were not trying to provide merely descriptive, historical statements of what ancient Israelites 'happened' to believe, leaving aside the question of truth or falsehood; they were trying to show what kind of God the OT bore witness to if it was read as a coherent whole. They were convinced that this God was congruous with the God witnessed to in the NT, and was indeed the true and living God, no mere creation of the human 'religious quest'. With these theologies we are back to reading the OT in order to discover the truth about God (or, better, to encounter God). If we read the OT with the interpretative categories of Eichrodt and von Rad, it will prove (they believed) to be a vehicle through which God is revealed as he truly is.

Of course the people in the days of the judges who thought God took pleasure in 'Holy War' and the ruthless destruction of Israel's enemies were mistaken. But this was not because they had a mistaken idea of what God was like. It was because they drew the wrong conclusions from an idea about God that in itself was perfectly true. What they read out of their religious belief in a God of covenant-loyalty, or a God who acted in the nation's saving history, was wrong – because they had not realized that such a God could not possibly demand violence and bloodshed. But the content of their belief, the idea of God's character to which Israel was committed, was and remains true. God really is a God who stands in a relationship of covenant to his people, giving and demanding loyalty; God really is committed to saving his people in their history.[7] So what the OT writers were positively trying to convey – the faith to which they were committed – is still true. What must be abandoned are some of the corollaries of this faith, some of the false conclusions people drew from it. But these do not detract from the truth of the faith itself.

For several reasons it is hard to feel completely happy with these approaches. It may be true that people in Israel perceived God in the way Eichrodt or von Rad believed; and it may be true that the way they perceived God is the way God really is. But one does not necessarily imply the other. Even if Eichrodt or von Rad gives us a completely satisfactory historical account of what 'Israel' believed, that still leaves wide open the question of what we ought to believe ourselves. Study of the actual assertions the OT makes about God, and of the family likeness between them all, seems to have reached the limit of its possibilities in the magisterial work of these two scholars. But it still leaves us unable to answer the question we began with – the question of what we can learn from the OT not about what people in biblical times thought about God, but about what God is actually like.

## V

Eichrodt and von Rad, for all their differences, began from what the OT says explicitly about God and his relation to Israel, the human race, the created world. But there remains the possibility of concentrating more on the assumptions underlying what the various biblical writers say. This area was the main concern of a number of biblical scholars of the 1950s and 1960s, whose work came to be known collectively as the Biblical Theology Movement.[8] In many books from this movement, the unity of the OT was perceived as being less a matter of agreement among all its writers in what they asserted, and more a feature of their underlying thought-patterns.[9] For example, 'biblical theology' agreed with von Rad in placing 'history' at the centre of the OT witness. But von Rad saw 'saving history' as a way in which Israel deliberately gave a shape and pattern to its existence; it was part of Israel's faith, something to which Israelites consciously committed themselves. For biblical theology, on the other hand, the ancient Israelites simply saw the world in terms of historical movement, and their God was a God whose whole mode of being was historical, whose nature was to be actively involved in human history. The idea was simply embedded in Israelite thought processes. The fact of Yahweh's involvement in history was presupposed throughout the whole OT.

Sometimes scholars from this school of thought went so far as to argue that a distinctively Hebraic way of thinking was built into the structures of the Hebrew language itself. For example, it was pointed out that the word we translate as 'truth' in the OT derives from a Hebrew verb that usually has the meaning 'be firm', 'be steadfast'. From this it was argued that 'truth', for the Israelites, was not a matter of intellectual conviction or objective proof, but of personal commitment and confidence.[10] 'To believe' in the OT would then mean not to think that some statement is true (to believe that . . .), but to commit oneself to something or someone, to put one's trust in something (to believe in . . .). Often the point was made that there was a great contrast between, on the one hand, Hebrew culture and Hebrew assumptions about reality – which tended to highlight personal commitment and involvement – and on the other hand western philosophies (deriving ultimately from Greek thought), with their emphasis on intellectual knowledge and objective, rational thought. 'Truth' was one of a number of terms that seemed to fit this distinction; 'love',[11] 'time',[12] and 'body'[13] were others.

Biblical theology, then, was a way of understanding the OT and its importance for the Christian reader that looked behind the text, and tried to grasp the basic ideas and categories of thought with which Israel worked. The Christian was supposed to learn to 'think Hebraically'. This did not mean trying to accept all that the OT asserted about God – for instance, it did not mean believing all the details of the exodus as the OT describes them. But it did mean seeing the world in the way Israel saw it, and in that way encountering Israel's God, who is still the God Christians worship.

The Biblical Theology Movement itself is now largely dead in the academic world, but its influence lives on in all sorts of subtle ways. The contrast between Hebrew and Greek modes of thought, and the conviction that Christian theology should prefer the former, is still widespread. It is still suggested that the main function of the OT in theology is as a source of 'concepts', 'ideas', or 'themes'. Biblical studies are sometimes taught, at both school and university level, in terms of 'biblical ways of thinking', and this owes much to the 'biblical theologians'. Sometimes the OT is referred to as a 'resource' from which ideas such as covenant, divine action in history, righteousness or faith can be drawn out and used in formulating Christian theology or grounding Christian ethics. Because it is difficult for Christians to turn directly to what the OT says as a source of information about the nature or will of God, people want to find other ways in which it can nevertheless continue to be fruitful for theology. Biblical theology provided the means of doing this, because it suggested that the real focus of revelation or religious truth within the OT lay in the Hebrew mentality to which it bore witness; and it recommended that modern believers should adjust their own way of thinking to fit in with this.

Again, however, we may feel uneasy. It is not clear why religious truth should be sought at the level of underlying assumptions or concepts rather than at the level of conscious belief. One way of putting this is to say that biblical theology helps us to dig in the OT, as in a mine, for styles of thinking or basic concepts that might be useful in constructing a living faith; but once the concepts have been extracted, the texts themselves are discarded like slag. Biblical theology shows us how to *process* the OT text, but not how to *read* it. It sees the theological value of the OT as located in underlying thought-patterns, rather than in the actual books of the OT as we now have them.

There is a problem in any suggestion that religious truth is to be found at the level of concepts rather than of assertions. In itself, after all, a concept such as 'divine activity in history' is religiously neutral. What interests the believer is not so much *that* God acts, but *how* God acts. It is small comfort to be told that it is God's nature to do things, if we are not told what sort of things he does. We are faced with a familiar problem: it is of no use to commend certain categories as 'biblical' or 'Hebraic', or to insist that the 'real' meaning of the OT belongs at a level below that of propositions, when what the ordinary reader of the OT is looking for is theological *truth*. It may be the case that we shall understand the theology of the biblical writers better by grasping the difference between Hebrew mentality and modern thought-modes, but that does not help us to know whether or not the biblical writers were correct in what they actually said about God. The OT cannot provide its own validation; we need to know what authority it has, before our improved interpretative tools will take us any further towards· using it in the quest for knowledge about or of God. Biblical theology is quite defensible in principle as another way of looking at the text, but it is no more of a solution to the problem we began with than are the OT theologies of Eichrodt or von Rad.

## VI

There have been important developments since the work of von Rad. One has been the emphasis on the 'canonical' shape of the OT that we find in the work of Brevard S. Childs.[14] For all their interest in finding a system in OT theology, Eichrodt and von Rad (and still more the biblical theologians) seem to Childs too historical in their emphasis. They work not with the text exactly as we find it when we open a Bible, but with reconstructed entities lying (or thought to lie) behind it: hypothetical sources, the 'authentic' utterances of prophets, social institutions whose existence is inferred from the text. Childs argues that we should turn away from all these historical hypotheses and interpret the text as it is, since it is the text as it is that the synagogue and the Church have 'canonized'. In church we hear readings from 'the book of Isaiah', 'the first book of Kings', not from 'oracles many scholars think go back to Isaiah' or from 'a partly historical account of the reign of Josiah'. OT theologies, for Childs, should not join in the reconstructive work of biblical historians, but should concentrate on the Bible in its canonical shape. Theology is communicated through the way the canon is arranged and articulated, not through the results of literary excavation, as it were. By contrast with historical criticism, Childs thinks it makes sense to ask what 'the Bible' says about this or that theological or ethical issue: in some ways this seems like a return to a 'pre-critical' approach to the text, but it is really a sophisticated attempt to be 'post-critical' – to learn from what biblical criticism has discovered, but insist that beyond it there remain questions about the authority and meaning of the Bible for Christians today. Childs' work is like that of Eichrodt and von Rad in that it sees the Bible thematically, with themes – covenant, Messiah, law – cutting across the various types of literature in their different periods. But the themes are those that emerge from the text itself on a careful reading; they are not concepts lying beneath the surface of the text and needing to be dug out by historical criticism.

A rather similar motivation lies behind the attempts made in recent years to present a theology of the whole Bible, Old and New Testament alike, which in the heyday of historical criticism was felt to be impossible because the material in the two Testaments was too disparate.[15] The work of Hartmut Gese has shown that there are still interesting possibilities for a 'pan-biblical' theology: indeed, he wants to include the Apocrypha within the Bible and see it too as fruitful for theological enquiry. Partly, however, this represents a continuing historical interest, for his rationale for including the Apocrypha is that it contains books that bridge the historical gap between the Old Testament and the New, rather than (though this would also be a valid reason) that the apocryphal books are part of the canon for the Catholic and Orthodox churches. Gese has rightly seen that some of the connections between Old and New Testaments discovered by the biblical theologians have lasting validity, showing that there is to some extent a biblical 'thought world'. The OT and the NT must not be forced into the same mould, but equally there is no reason why genuine resemblances between them should not be registered.

The last decade has seen particularly strong attacks on the enterprise of OT theology, from two different points of view. Some Jewish biblical scholars have denounced it as a forcible Christianizing of the OT. Jews, they argue, are not interested in the 'theology' of the Bible, if this means theological constructions based on biblical texts that can be shown to interconnect with themes in the NT.[16] It is not clear whether a Jewish 'Hebrew Bible Theology' would escape this attack, or whether it would be seen as a Jewish capitulation to the Christian belief that there is 'theology' in the text, where Judaism has more commonly seen 'Torah' (ethical teaching). In any case, few Jewish scholars have ever felt the need to produce such a theology. There can be little doubt that the classic theologies of Eichrodt and von Rad do have a Christian agenda, even though their treatment of the OT text is not a deliberate reading in of Christian ideas. Writing an OT theology on the hypothesis that the NT had never come into being would be an interesting academic exercise, and one that might well uncover previously unnoticed themes in the OT. It could also have a useful 'ecumenical' dimension.

The other main attack on OT theology has come from Rainer Albertz, who maintains that it is time for the discipline to give way to the study of the history of Israelite religion, and has tried to demonstrate this in a major two-volume study.[17] Religion in ancient Israel of course had 'theological' elements – people believed certain things about the God (or god or gods) they worshipped. But it is only one element alongside social and historical aspects of the practice of religion, and should not be elevated to a crowning role in our study of the OT. Furthermore, in many periods of Israelite history we are simply ignorant of the beliefs people held, and in every period we must remember that the same set of beliefs is unlikely to have been held by everyone. Albertz is not against a sketch of the 'family likeness' within Israelite religion, but is strongly opposed to synthesizing attempts that overlook the minute historical detail to which the OT bears witness. In his view there is a certain naivety in much work on OT theology, and any future theology of the OT will have to take his sharp criticisms into account.

## VII

Can we make any progress in thinking about OT theology? We could ask: What is the *goal* of OT theology as a branch of biblical study? Perhaps we should think of it not so much as a matter of extracting information from the OT, or of summarizing its theological content, but more as providing explanations that will help us to read and use the OT with more understanding. The OT is not primarily a source of *information*, either about God or about other people's ideas of God; it is primarily a collection of various kinds of *literature* whose main themes and subject-matter are religious. And with literature, which in this respect is very different from a textbook or a catechism, we cannot extract the 'message' and then discard the wrappings; the message is inextricably bound up with the way in which it is presented. The role of OT theology is to help us to understand this particular collection of literature by explaining the various concepts it uses, the kind of God it presupposes, the ways in which its authors thought this God had acted, and what they believed he had commanded. There should be no thought in our minds that the author of a theology of the OT tells us what the OT *really* means more clearly than the text itself does. The task of OT theology is the purely ancillary one of helping us to understand the categories and ideas with which the OT text works. No reading of critical literature can be a substitute for reading the OT text for ourselves;

and when we do read it, this is not in order to 'extract' information from it, but to come, through it, to grasp the realities of which its authors speak.

Thus, for example, an OT theology can help us to understand what idea of God is presupposed by the Psalms, and can list the attributes the psalmists saw him as possessing: power, glory, uniqueness, transcendence, mercy, and so on. It can make these ideas more precise than would be possible on a simple reading of the text, and can fill them out by showing how they are dealt with in other parts of the OT, and how they differ from modern ideas that may seem similar. But a psalm is not rightly seen as designed to 'teach' us these things, for a psalm is a text the worshipping community sings *to* God, not a communication addressed to the worshipper, either by God or by anyone else. The only proper way to 'use' a psalm, in the end, is to sing it, not to study it as a possible source of information. Similar things might be said about the narrative texts that make up more than half the OT. Studies of the theological beliefs of ancient Israel will help us to read them with understanding, but they were not written to provide information about these theological beliefs; they were written in order to tell a story or recount a history. In this sense the theology of the historical books is a secondary concern. Although God figures in the stories, and they do not make sense except on the basis of various beliefs about him, they are not designed to tell the reader things about God, but rather to narrate events from a particular point of view. We discover what their authors are trying to say by reading their account, not by abstracting the theology embedded in it and discarding the framework.

The practical effect of these suggestions is to make rather more than is made in the OT theologies discussed so far of the distinction between the OT text on the one hand, and the life and culture of ancient Israel that constitute its background on the other. It does not make sense to distinguish them in such a way that the OT is read in a sort of vacuum. It must be read against its background. Much recent OT study has rightly stressed that most books in the OT were in any case not produced by authors in our sense at all, but are the crystallization of the thinking of the community at large. But we still ought to keep in mind that there is a distinction to be made between the OT text and those who wrote it on the one hand, and the great mass of Israelites on the other (this is the point made so sharply by

Albertz). Important though it is to be aware of the context of ancient Israelite life and belief against which OT books make sense, it is equally important to remember that they may not be merely an expression of beliefs held commonly or widely in Israel. The OT is, in effect, the official version of ancient Israel's life and thought, the classic formulations of the community's faith that it chose to hand on to future generations (one of the points made by Childs). The task of elucidating the background of religious belief that enables us to make sense of this text is therefore not the same as the task of expounding the text itself. The OT theologian can be usefully employed in the first of these tasks – and the latter part of this book will be given over to OT theology in this sense. But the second task, the exposition of the text, is (like all exposition of texts) not a matter of an expositor constructing a system. Its aim is to enable the reader to hear the text itself. On this level, biblical scholarship does not provide raw materials for systematic theologians to use by extracting the theology from the OT text. Instead, it enables systematic theologians (or religious believers) to hear more clearly what the text is saying, and to construct their theology, or practise their faith, as those to whom the Bible has been enabled to communicate its own message in its own way.


# VII

So there are two purposes a book on the theology of the OT could usefully serve. One is to provide us with all sorts of background information that will help us to understand the religious tradition within which the OT writings belong. Because these texts come from a rather remote culture, we need expert help in understanding the shared assumptions with which they work, and in terms of which they make sense. As a matter of fact, it is at this level that Eichrodt's *Theology* functions best, even though it claims to do something rather different. It reconstructs the religious thought of the ancient Israelites (for which, of course, the OT provides the great bulk of evidence), and thereby prepares us to read the text with more understanding; for more up-to-date accounts of the historical data, Albertz provides an indispensable addition.

Another way in which we can approach the matter is by trying to analyse the actual theological statements made in various OT books, and to find ways of describing their theological atmosphere. Then we can go on to synthesize the results (if it proves that the family likeness among the various books is strong enough to justify this), so as to produce a summary of the theological impression a careful reading of the whole OT is likely to make. This comes nearer to what von Rad was attempting (and Childs, in some ways, is his heir). Either way of writing an OT theology is likely to be useful to the student, and both seem to be legitimate approaches. Our discussion has suggested a few pitfalls, however, and we will conclude by saying a little about them.

First, the distinction between the two kinds of project needs to be kept clear, even if in practice we want to say that the results of each are congruent with those of the other. A description of the religious beliefs of Israel in different periods is not the same as an analysis of the leading themes or topics of the OT, and there is no direct line from one to the other. Both Eichrodt's and von Rad's works – and this is also true of books produced under the influence of biblical theology – tend to suffer from a failure to be clear which of these two things they are talking about. Both are needed, but they need to be kept distinct.

Second, we need to know whether we are trying to describe what was believed in Israel or stated in the OT on the one hand, or to say what is in fact the case, as a matter of theological truth, on the other. Again, religious believers will see some correlation between the two, though different people will have different ideas about how close the correlation is. Any doctrine of scriptural inspiration will include a belief that it is somehow providential that we have the Scriptures we have, that God wants us to understand him by means of these particular texts. This will entail that the existence of various shared assumptions and beliefs in ancient Israel, which were necessary if those texts were to be possible, was also in some sense intended by God. (Spelling out 'somehow' and 'in some sense' here is the major task faced by any doctrine of inspiration.) But this is essentially separate from the purely empirical questions of what people in fact believed, or what the text actually says. Our answer to the first question must not be allowed to colour our reconstruction of OT theology, in either of the senses just discussed, so as (for example) to make us see this as a gradual development from worse to better ideas of God, if the evidence does not point in this direction. The type of material the OT contains is not

ideally suited to analysis in terms of the 'idea of God' it is trying
to convey. It functions more obliquely than that, by telling
stories, singing praises and speaking in aphorisms about life;
and if it is to be fruitful for modern theologians and believers,
then this will be more because these people listen carefully to
what it is saying, in the way it chooses to say it, than because
they can reconstruct from it the beliefs of its authors or the
religious experiences of the community that lies behind them. A
modern interest in 'using' the OT in Christian theology should
not be allowed to influence our understanding of what it says, in
its own right.

Third, nothing is gained by exaggerating the unity either of the
OT or of the religious assumptions and beliefs of ancient Israelites.
As we have seen, neither Eichrodt nor von Rad was trying to
claim that the OT spoke with an absolutely single voice, though
the Biblical Theology Movement did tend in this direction. But
any synthesizing work on OT theology is apt to blow up the
admitted family likeness of the material into a virtual identity of
content, and to speak as though there were beliefs held by 'Israel'
as such that remained constant throughout the 'OT period' –
an idea against which Albertz has protested effectively. Against
this it is surely right to say that the OT contains a variety of
theologies, and attests a variety of religious perceptions and
convictions, varying with period, with social group, even
perhaps with geographical location. It is perfectly reasonable to
look for unifying themes and common features that account for
the fact that this is manifestly the literature of a single broad
tradition. But sometimes OT scholars first locate what seems to
them the 'centre' of the OT, or of the religion of Israel, and then
reject certain parts of the text as 'not truly Israelite': the frequent
treatment of the wisdom books as uncharacteristic of Israelite
thought is the most striking case of this.[18] When OT theology is
written in this way, it ceases to be descriptive of what is actually
the case, and starts to issue directives about what ought to be the
case. Often we find that strains of theological thought are being
described as 'central' to the OT because they chime in best with
a particular scholar's own ideas of theological truth. When this
happens, the discipline of OT theology ceases to serve readers of
the Bible and becomes their master, forcing them to read the text
from a standpoint artificially imposed upon it. The only remedy
is for students to insist on reading the text for themselves, not
accepting any generalizations about its central themes or

insights unless they can find evidence for them in their own reading.

## NOTES

1 Rainer Albertz has recently argued that there should be no discipline of OT theology that tries to be anything more than the history of Israelite religion.

2 *Winding Quest* is the title of an excellent abridged OT for children by A. T. Dale (London, Oxford University Press, 1972; Wilton, Morehouse-Barlow, 1973). It does not put forward the approach I am describing here – its title simply provides a useful phrase. A winding quest approach is common in school biblical studies syllabuses.

3 A particularly clear discussion of this can be found in Gerd Theissen, *Biblical Faith: An Evolutionary Approach* (London, SCM Press, 1984).

4 W. Eichrodt, *Theology of the Old Testament* (London, SCM, 1967; Philadelphia, Westminster Press, 1967).

5 G. von Rad, *Old Testament Theology* (Edinburgh, Oliver & Boyd, 1962–5; New York, Harper & Row, 1962–5.

6 For example, A. Phillips, *Deuteronomy*, Cambridge Bible Commentary on the New English Bible (Cambridge, Cambridge University Press, 1974).

7 As this implies, the theologies of Eichrodt and von Rad differ, but are not incompatible.

8 On 'biblical theology', see B.S. Childs, *Biblical Theology in Crisis* (Philadelphia, Westminster Press, 1970).

9 See N. H. Snaith, *The Distinctive Ideas of the Old Testament* (London, Epworth Press, 1944; New York, Schocken Books, 1964); G.E. Wright, *God Who Acts* (London, SCM, 1958).

10 See the discussion of this approach in J. Barr, *The Semantics of Biblical Language* (Oxford, Oxford University Press, 1961), pp. 161–205.

11 See for example the classic study by A. Nygren, *Agape and Eros* (London, SPCK, 1957).

12 See O. Cullmann, *Christ and Time* (London, SCM, 1957).

13 See J.A.T. Robinson, *The Body: A Study in Pauline Theology* (London, SCM, 1952).

14 See B.S. Childs, *Biblical Theology in Crisis*; *Introduction to the Old Testament as Scripture* (Philadelphia, Fortress Press, 1984); *Biblical Theology of the Old and New Testaments* (London, SCM, 1992).

15 See H. Gese, *Vom Sinai zum Zion* (Munich, Chr. Kaiser, 1974); *Zur biblischen Theologie* (Munich, Chr. Kaiser, 1977); and the survey of 'pan-biblical' theology in M. Oeming, *Gesamtbiblische Theologien der Gegenwart* (Stuttgart, Kohlhammer, 1985).

16 See J.D. Levenson, *The Hebrew Bible, the Old Testament, and Historical Criticism: Jews and Christians in Biblical Studies* (Philadelphia, Westminster, 1993).

17 See R. Albertz, *A History of Israelite Religion in the Old Testament Period* (2 vols, London, SCM, 1994).

18 Cf. H.D. Preuss, *Old Testament Theology* (Edinburgh, T. & T. Clark, 1995).

## FURTHER READING

Albertz, R., *A History of Israelite Religion in the Old Testament Period* (2 vols, London, SCM, 1994).

Clements, R.E., *Old Testament Theology: A Fresh Approach* (London, Marshall, Morgan and Scott, 1978).

Goldingay, J., *Theological Diversity and the Authority of the Old Testament* (Grand Rapids, Eerdmans, 1987).

Levenson, J.D., *The Hebrew Bible, the Old Testament, and Historical Criticism: Jews and Christians in Biblical Studies* (Philadelphia, Westminster/John Knox, 1993).

Ollenburger, B.C., Martens, E.A., and Hasel, G.F. (eds.), *The Flowering of Old Testament Theology: A Reader in Twentieth-Century Old Testament Theology, 1930–90* (Winona Lake, Eisenbrauns, 1992).

Reventlow, H., *Problems of Old Testament Theology in the Twentieth Century* (London, SCM, 1985).

Schmidt, W.H., *The Faith of the Old Testament* (Philadelphia, Westminster, 1983).

Spriggs, D.G., *Two Old Testament Theologies* (London, SCM, 1974).

Whybray, R.N., 'Old Testament Theology – A Non-Existent Beast?', in B.P. Thompson (ed.), *Scripture: Meaning and Method* (Hull, Hull University, 1987), pp. 168–80.

# 7

## Approaches to Ethics in the Old Testament

### JOHN BARTON

### I

> Then Samuel said, 'Bring here to me Agag the king of the Ama-
> lekites.' And Agag came to him cheerfully. Agag said, 'Surely
> the bitterness of death is past.' And Samuel said, 'As your
> sword has made women childless, so shall your mother be child-
> less among women.' And Samuel hewed Agag in pieces before
> the LORD in Gilgal. (1 Samuel 15.32–3 RSV)

This passage perfectly epitomizes, in many people's minds, the
ethics of the Old Testament. A bloodthirsty God exacts
vengeance, and will not be moved by entreaty; the agents of God
must close their hearts to any natural human pity. This is the
kind of thing that people have in mind when they say that
someone has 'an Old Testament attitude' to morality. Yet it is also
from the OT that we have what is often regarded as a perfect
summary of Christian moral conduct:

> What does the LORD require of you but to do justice, and to
> love kindness, and to walk humbly with your God? (Micah 6.8)

And it is in the OT that the 'two great commandments' of the law,
love for God and for one's neighbour, are to be found
(Deuteronomy 6.5 and Leviticus 19.18, cf. Mark 12.29–31). An
initial dip into the ethical ideas of the OT might suggest that
they are merely chaotic. It is hardly surprising that there are so
few books on OT ethics, if the OT material swings so wildly

between extremes. Perhaps the OT has no really coherent message on this subject . . .

One of the purposes of this chapter will indeed be to suggest that the OT enshrines a variety of ethical points of view, and that there is no more one 'ethics of the OT' than there is one 'theology of the OT'. Nevertheless, in the later sections of the chapter we shall go on to suggest that the picture is not one of total chaos, but that certain clear lines may be discerned. Before we can present either side of the case properly, however, we need to make it much clearer what is meant by the rather vague phrase 'Old Testament ethics'.

## II

'Old Testament ethics' can refer to two related but distinct things. Sometimes the study of 'OT ethics' means the study of the historical development of ideas about morality, or of actual moral conduct, in ancient Israel. In this sense, to study the ethics of the OT is like studying the ethics of medieval Europe, or classical Greece or modern China. Such a study is not necessarily 'merely' historical. As we saw when discussing the study of religious belief in ancient Israel, Christians are likely to believe that ancient Israelites were in certain important ways in touch with God, so that what they thought about moral obligation is of more than purely antiquarian interest to us. Nevertheless, it *is* historical, primarily: it is a matter of reconstructing, on the basis of the evidence provided by the OT text and any other evidence that may be available, how people in ancient Israel behaved, and how they thought they were supposed to behave. Such a study yields some interesting results, which are the despair of anyone trying to reconstruct the ethical 'system' of ancient Israel; for they are very diverse, and suggest that ancient Israelite society was richly varied in its attitudes and practices.

But the second thing we might be doing in studying OT ethics is to take the OT essentially as a book that forms part of Christian Scripture, and to ask what, in its finished form, it has to say to us about ethical issues. As we noted in chapter 6, despite its great variety there is also a strong family likeness about the OT in all its parts. It represents not just a random sample or cross-section of the beliefs of ancient Israelites, but a sort of official version of these beliefs – an orthodox presentation of Israelite religion and ethics as Israel, in the last centuries before Christ, wished these to be understood. At this level it does provide a reasonably unified and clear ethical system, though of such a high degree of generality that it would be hard to apply it in practice in resolving any particular ethical dilemma. It is more a matter of a common flavour or atmosphere, a certain style of approach to moral questions. But if we are studying OT ethics in this second sense, there is far less need to be pessimistic about our chances of having something coherent and unified to show for our labours.

The fatal mistake is not be clear in our mind which of these two types of enquiry we are engaged in. Quite often discussions of what the OT teaches on a particular moral question do not make this necessary distinction, and shift uneasily between historical questions about whether (say) the Patriarchs recognized or observed certain moral rules, or what the prophets thought Israelites of their day ought to do, and questions about what God is telling us through the OT that *we* ought to do. Of course, there may be routes that will take us from one to the other. But it is muddled thinking not to see that the questions are distinct. The OT as a finished book on the one hand, and the multiplicity of ancient Israelites about whom it informs us in various ways on the other, are not at all the same thing, and little progress can be made so long as they are confused. It might be helpful to describe the two areas that will need discussion as 'Ethics in ancient Israel' and 'The Ethics of the OT'. In what follows we shall examine each separately.

## III

## *Ethics in ancient Israel*

Any historical study of ethical conduct, norms and systems in ancient Israel is bound to be highly complex, for the OT provides material from which to reconstruct the life and thought of a whole nation over a period of about a thousand years; and we could hardly expect that everything would have remained the same throughout this period, or that the various different social groups within the nation would necessarily have agreed among themselves even within one part of it. Even a cursory examination shows that there is a great variety reflected even within the limited material that actually found its way into the

OT, and we can only guess at the much greater bulk of material from which this was selected. By way of illustration, we shall examine three questions in the realm of ethics, on all of which the OT contains indications that there were many different opinions and traditions in Israel. These are:

- actual moral norms;
- the basis of ethics;
- the motives and incentives for moral conduct.

## MORAL NORMS

It is fairly obvious to any careful reader of the OT that the accepted norms of conduct in ancient Israel varied a good deal. To put it more precisely, we may say that the sorts of conduct people thought to be right can only be described if we take into account at least two variable factors. One of these is time. There are a number of areas of moral concern where we have to reckon with change and development from century to century in the long history of Israel. For example, the OT never formally repudiates polygamy, but monogamy certainly became the more usual arrangement in Israel in later times – exactly when, we do not know. Many customs that, it seems, had been comparatively unimportant or even non-existent in the period before the Babylonian exile of the sixth century BCE, moved into the centre of ethical interest in the post-exilic age. Among these may be mentioned sabbath observance, circumcision and the rigorous keeping of the food laws. All these are 'markers' of Judaism that, though they were probably practised at least by some before the Exile, had not then been a matter of active commitment because at that time there was an Israelite state (organized on political rather than narrowly religious lines) to maintain the distinction between Israelite and non-Israelite. Some norms of ethical conduct come and go in such a way that one cannot easily speak of development, still less progress, but only of variation. For example, the belief that Israel had a moral duty to wipe out pagans who worshipped other gods, and who tried to seduce or coerce Israelites into doing the same, flourishes in some periods, but seems to be almost forgotten in others. It does not seem ever to have been officially repudiated, but in times of security and peace we do not hear of its being put into action. Some scholars think that in Deuteronomy, where it is quite prominent (see Deuteronomy 12.29–31; 13.1–18), it is to be understood chiefly as a call to total allegiance to Yahweh rather than as a literal command to kill those who worship gods other than Yahweh. Whatever may have been the intention of Deuteronomy, it is clear that as an actual incentive to action such laws were a dead letter for much of the time. In some ways the period from about 200 BCE down to the age of the New Testament saw more of a resurgence of this idea than many of the previous centuries, and in a curious way the age of the Maccabees reaches back across the years to touch the period of the Judges (at least as that is reported in the OT). Other parts of the moral code, by contrast, seem to have remained fairly static, and this is true of many areas of conduct where Israel shared in a general ethical tradition common to much of the ancient Near East. Such might be a number of the issues dealt with in the Ten Commandments – murder, theft, adultery – though the way in which the community dealt with breaches of such norms may well have varied from time to time.

Less obvious, perhaps, but arguably even more important, is the variable of social group. Comparatively little can be said with confidence about the sociology of ancient Israel: though we can speak loosely of 'tribes', 'families' and 'clans', and of social stratification in terms of 'rulers', 'administrators', 'scribes', of 'priests', 'prophets' and 'wise men', we have only quite rough-and-ready standards by which to distinguish and describe these various groups. Nevertheless, even from an OT that has plainly been edited to express the attitudes of the official religious leadership in the post-exilic age, and to smooth out the evidence of dissenting voices, it is clear that in many periods there were sharp divisions of emphasis, and even straightforward disagreements, between different groups in Israel over many ethical issues. The pre-exilic prophets consistently speak as though the ethical norms to which they are trying to recall the nation are despised or rejected by the nation's leaders. (See, for example, Isaiah 1.15–17; 5.8–23; Jeremiah 7.5–15; 22.1–19; Amos 6.1–7.) If the leaders modelled their lives more on the patterns provided in books such as Proverbs than on the lines suggested by the prophets, it is not surprising that there seems to have been little common ground. As in our discussion of OT theology, so here we must be careful not to ignore the clear family likeness even between groups as opposed as prophets and rulers appear sometimes to have been. But the differences also are real enough to deter us from speaking of 'the Israelite ethic', as though they represented merely minor variations on an identical theme. In a much later period, as we know from studies of NT background, Judaism had many sects and religious groups of diverse character; and though it makes sense to call them all 'Jewish', since all evinced a basic adherence to the law, the focus of their moral concern varied very widely. We can speak of the ethics of the Qumran community, or of the Pharisees, or of the high-priestly party.

One of the problems in trying to produce a *history* of ethics in Israel is that in most periods we do not have evidence for more than a few of the various social strata that made up 'Israel', and often our evidence is for different groups in different periods. One can easily imagine how difficult it would be to write a history of ethics in England if our evidence for the seventeenth century was entirely composed of the writings of philosophers, for the eighteenth of records of parliamentary debates, for the nineteenth of popular novels, and for the twentieth of school reports. Yet something not too unlike this is the situation that confronts us in the OT. It is all too easy to speak, for example, of the post-exilic age as a time of 'increasing legalism' (on the strength of the books of Ezra and Nehemiah and material in the Pentateuch, especially Leviticus) that probably reached its final form during or after the Exile. But the fact is that we have, in these books, evidence of what the priests were teaching in the early post-exilic period, and little evidence of what other groups then believed; whereas, for the pre-exilic age, we have a great deal of prophetic material, but hardly anything we can confidently ascribe to priestly circles. For all we know they may have been just as 'legalistic' before the Exile as after it: there is simply no evidence one way or the other. So far, then, as actual moral norms recognized in Israel are concerned, we can speak of some general tendencies, so long as we stay at a fairly non-specific level; but when we come down to details, the material at our disposal dissolves into a fascinatingly varied, but quite unsystematic jumble.

## THE BASIS OF ETHICS

Ancient Israel possessed nothing that could be described as 'moral philosophy' – the attempt to work out systematically the basis on which ethics rests, and to clarify why it is that moral imperatives or norms have the binding character that people attribute to them. In this sense, the OT is not speculative or philosophical literature. Nevertheless, it does make sense to ask what in ancient Israel was thought or felt (perhaps at a fairly inarticulate level) to be the underlying basis of morality. The short answer most readers of the OT would give to this question is 'God', and this would certainly be right for most of the thinking that is attested in the OT. There is, it is true, a certain amount of evidence within the OT that some Israelites thought in terms of merely human *conventions* in certain areas of morality, rather than of divine authority: much of the so-called 'wisdom' literature, such as Proverbs, has this character, and expressions such as 'Such things are not done in Israel' (2 Samuel 13.12) may point in the same direction. Furthermore, most people no doubt gave little thought to the question whether morality derived from God or not! But by and large the OT registers only religious attitudes to morality, and this shows that, at least for those who produced it, God was very much at the centre of ethical obligation.

To say this, however, is not to say all that can be said about the basis of ethics in Israel, for morality can be religious in more than one way. Perhaps the simplest form of religious morality is found where people think that ethics is a matter of doing what God tells them. Either they devise ways of discovering what God's will is (through oracles or prophets or accredited teachers such as priests), or else they interpret laws and precepts that are actually in force as expressions of the will of God, and claim that they have been revealed at some specific time. (Perhaps this is currently so; we are not concerned here either to support or rule out this possibility.) The OT contains plenty of material that shows such a view to have been common in Israel at many periods. Some such model is obviously present in the story of Moses receiving the law on Sinai (Exodus 19–23), and in accounts of people asking priests or prophets to rule on difficult questions of morality (see Haggai 2.10–19); and the idea of the covenant, as a book like Deuteronomy presents it, is that Israel must perform the obligations God lays on it as the terms of his contract with the nation.

On the other hand, the wisdom literature, as we see it in Proverbs, looks at morality in a rather different way, even when it does try to relate it to God. Here we find fewer references to God as the giver of laws or moral norms, and more interest in presenting morality as a matter of fitting one's life to the orders and patterns observable in the world that is God's creation. This has some affinities with what the western tradition of moral philosophy has usually called natural law. There is a good example of this way of thinking in the book of Job (31.13–15), where Job acknowledges that he has a duty to act justly towards his slaves because they, like him, were made by the same God and therefore share the same nature. This is very different from the idea that we find repeatedly in Deuteronomy, where the Israelites have an obligation to be kind to slaves because God *commands* them to be, as part of their side of the covenant relationship with him. Indeed, this example brings out another way in which Israelite writers sometimes seek to express the basis of human morality; for Deuteronomy also argues that the Israelites should be kind to slaves because *God* is kind to them, as is proved by the fact that he took pity on their own forebears when they were slaves in Egypt – see Deut. 15.15. Here an appeal is being made to what we might call the 'imitation of God' as the foundation of ethics, an idea that Martin Buber[1] argued was fundamental to the OT, though there are not in fact many passages where we can be confident that it occurs. Even when it does, it does not necessarily mean that a very exalted or sublime kind of morality is being commanded. After all, the quotation with which this chapter began was in a sense concerned with the imitation of God! If God is seen as one who exacts bloody retribution, then the idea that ethics is the imitation of God may well lead to an 'inhuman' standard of morality. On the other hand, insights into morality may come to be reflected back onto the understanding of God himself, so that people come to say: *We* must not exact vengeance, but rather show forgiveness; how then can we believe *God* to be less merciful than we know we ought to be ourselves? There is a discussion of this sort of reasoning below, on p. 129. We can say, then, that there are at least three models or 'theories' of God's role in relation to human moral obligation that the OT shows to have been current in ancient Israel: obedience to God's commandments, conformity to the patterns and orders of the world, and imitation of God's own character and conduct. These can, indeed, be merged in various ways, as we shall see; but at least we seem to be justified in saying that on the question of the basis of ethics, as in the area of particular moral norms, the OT bears witness to a rich and varied world of thought. In recommending various courses of action as morally right, the people who produced the literature of the OT were able to draw on a number of different approaches, and these, presumably, found some echo in the minds of the Israelites to whom their work was addressed. Once again, then, we seem to need quite a pluralistic presentation if we are to do justice to ethics in ancient Israel.

## MOTIVES AND INCENTIVES TO MORAL CONDUCT

Much the same needs to be said of another area that interests students of ethics: the question of sticks and carrots, of incentives to act well and threats of the consequences of acting badly. What did people in Israel think would happen to them if they behaved wrongly; what motives did they have for behaving rightly? Here we shall naturally be concerned mostly with the evidence provided by those books that seek to admonish or instruct the readers, especially the so-called 'law books' of the Pentateuch. In these we find once more a rich variety of approaches – particularly well discussed in Eichrodt's *Theology of the Old Testament*, vol. ii, chapter 22.

One might classify the incentives to moral conduct in the OT very roughly by saying that some look to the future, some to the past, and some to the present. Incentives are, in our way of thinking, most often a matter of holding out some promise of future reward or threat of future punishment, and this kind of incentive is certainly plentiful in the OT too. The Ten Commandments contain one such: 'Honour your father and your mother, that your days may be long in the land.' The early collection of law generally known as the 'Book of the Covenant' or 'Covenant Code' (Exodus 21–23) has another: 'If you take your neighbour's garment in pledge, you shall restore it to him before the sun goes down . . . for if he cries to me, I will hear, for I am compassionate' (Exodus 22.25–7) – a barely-veiled threat to the would-be offender. The wisdom books also abound in such incentives – indeed, one of their major concerns is to urge that righteousness brings prosperity and unrighteousness disaster, even to the point where common sense is outraged.

But there is also often an appeal to the past, to the gratitude to God for what he has done that ought to prompt one to obey him or to order one's life in the right way. Deuteronomy is particularly rich in passages stressing this aspect: 'Your fathers went down to Egypt seventy persons, and now the LORD your God has made you as the stars of heaven for multitude; you shall therefore love the LORD your God, and keep his charge, his statutes and ordinances . . . ' (Deuteronomy 10.22–11.1). It also occurs, as we have already noted, in the injunction to be kind to slaves out of gratitude for God's kindness to Israel's ancestors when *they* were slaves; and in the Deuteronomic version of the fourth commandment: 'Observe the sabbath day, to keep it holy. . . . that your manservant and your maidservant may rest as well as you. You shall remember that you were a servant in the land of Egypt, and the LORD your God brought you out thence with a mighty hand and an outstretched arm . . .' (Deuteronomy 5.12–14).

Though it is perhaps slightly forced to speak of an incentive based on the *present*, we might describe in this way some of the OT passages that insist on the inherent moral beauty of God's laws as reason enough for keeping them. The law itself is a treasure the Israelite possesses by observing it, and what more could anyone ask? Psalm 119 is probably the best exposition of such a view in the OT: 'I opened my mouth, and drew in my breath for joy, for my delight was in thy commandments' (Psalm 119.131). But Deuteronomy, again, thinks along these lines: 'What great nation is there that has statutes and ordinances so righteous as all this law which I set before you this day? (Deuteronomy 4.8). The suggestion that the law is to be kept because it is inherently good – the kind of law that anyone in his senses would be only too pleased to have a chance of keeping – greatly stresses the goodness and reasonableness of the God who gives such a law. God is not an arbitrary tyrant, but knows what is best for his people; and this in itself is an incentive to do as he commands.

The OT, therefore, and still more the life of Israel that lies behind the OT, presents an enormously rich and varied range of attitudes towards ethics in its various aspects. Ethics in ancient Israel is a neglected subject, but one that deserves a great deal of attention.

## IV

## *The ethics of the Old Testament*

In discussing OT theology in Chapter 6, we saw that, when all allowances have been made for the diversity of actual theological assertions within the OT, and of religious beliefs in the society from which it derives, it still makes sense to ask about the overall character of the theological tradition the finished work enshrines.

The same is true for ethics. Before the rise of historical criticism, readers of the OT were far less aware than we are now of the diversity in its material; but this is far from meaning that they did not notice problems in reconciling one part with another, and in extracting any clear and consistent moral teaching from it. Yet, on the whole, they thought that the Scriptures of the OT had a 'general drift', which made it possible, with care, to see them as broadly supporting some ethical positions and ruling out others; and this is far from being a foolish or unreasonable approach to adopt. Our best course will be to go back to two of the areas we examined under the heading of 'Ethics in Ancient Israel', and see how they look when approached from the angle of the OT as a finished work, as part of Christian Scripture. We shall deal with moral norms and the basis of ethics.

## MORAL NORMS

The problem that we immediately face when we try to discover what actual moral principles or norms can be extracted from the OT is that the OT does not seem designed as a mine from which these things are meant to be extracted. Although it has long been customary for Christians to understand the OT as 'law'[2] (taken to mean something like 'regulations for living'), such an approach immediately faces the problem that rather little of the OT actually has the *form* of law. Large parts of it are composed of narrative, hymnody or prophecy, and the texts in which positive instructions are issued as to how people ought to live make up only a tiny fraction of the whole. Even though the Pentateuch is traditionally called 'the Law' (we shall examine this in the next section), this is clearly in a somewhat extended sense of the term, for even Leviticus and Deuteronomy, which contain primarily 'legal' or 'instructional' material, are given a narrative framework; while Genesis and Numbers are almost exclusively narrative, and contain scarcely anything that we would naturally call law at all. Both Judaism and Christianity have developed complex systems of interpretative method that would enable them to extract 'law' in the straightforward sense ('rules') from this heterogeneous collection of material. But, as with 'theology', it can be argued that it is false to the nature of the material to see it primarily as a quarry from which 'ethics' must be dug by whatever tools can be devised for the purpose. If it is to inform our ethical judgements, this will be because we allow our understanding of what it is saying *on its own terms* to work on our minds, as we face the issues on which we ourselves must make our own ethical decisions.

This certainly means that the quest for 'proof texts' will not serve our purpose, and this of course is true for any use of the OT that seeks to take critical study seriously. But on most ethical questions a proof-text approach is, in any case, of no use, since the evidence is conflicting. Texts can be assembled both in favour of and against polygamy, capital punishment, divorce and war. Notoriously, on one issue that is very hotly debated among Christians today, one can cite directly conflicting judgements from OT Scripture. This is the question whether armed resistance to lawfully constituted authority is justified in the name of ethical or religious principles. This issue clearly arises in the case of the bloody coup instigated by Elisha and accomplished by Jehu (2 Kings 9–10). The author of Kings applauds this as a work of loyalty to God; Hosea (1.4) condemns it utterly, and pronounces God's imminent vengeance for it. Once we resort to proof texts, all the diversity with which the previous section dealt becomes a source of confusion and despair.

But this masks the general problem of how we are to evaluate ethical ideas contained in material of such diverse character. Neither Kings nor Hosea, after all, is couched in the form of law or even of moral teaching: Kings is narrative, with occasional commentary inserted into it, and Hosea is prophecy, delivered for the occasion and not necessarily generalizable, as it would need to be if we were to build an ethical system on it.

To make any progress in the face of this difficulty we shall have to stand back a little further from the detail of the OT, and make rather more of the 'general drift' idea just mentioned in connection with older interpretations. Although much of the OT does not have the form of law, the principle that was at work in the process that led to its becoming 'Scripture', and being understood as in some way a single work, was certainly that readers should be able to derive profit, both religious and moral, from reading it in *all* its parts – not just those that directly contain words of prohibition or command. Most of the narratives do, either directly or incidentally, tend to establish some sorts of moral value as commendable and others as unacceptable. The prophetic books, and even the Psalms, though they do not lay down moral norms in the manner of a lawcode, can only be appreciated or assented to or used liturgically on the assumption of a broad general adherence to a moral tradition that (though it may not be easy to define) does have some distinctive content. For example: even if we did not have the laws (in Deuteronomy and elsewhere) actually forbidding certain types of orgiastic religious rites, it would be clear from reading the historical books that the 'official' theology these books present, as part of the canon of Scripture, is against such things. We may not be able to point to any particular text and say that it forbids such rites in a way that is plainly binding on the modern believer, but it is difficult to think that one could ascribe *any* kind of authority to the OT and still think that this was compatible with a religious practice that included orgies. It would immediately strike anyone who actually practised a religion that did include this element, that the OT, taken in its general drift, has an ethos into which it does not fit! To say, as we must, that there is enormous variety in the OT, that on some important issues it is deeply ambiguous, that much of it is not directly concerned with ethics anyway – all this is true; but it remains the case that the OT can only make coherent sense within a particular religious and ethical system, which can be specified and described, even if only in very general terms.

Sometimes there is real disagreement within the OT – as on the question of whether the pagan world stands under God's judgement, and should be rejected and even physically attacked (compare 1 Samuel 15 with Jonah). Yet we can sometimes see that the disagreement takes place against a background of certain common assumptions. 1 Samuel and Jonah both assume that Yahweh is a God who demands total allegiance and whose purposes must not be resisted by human beings, even though the practical conclusions they draw from this are plainly opposed. Hindus might well be struck by the fact that both works assume that it is a matter of the highest importance to worship the right God and to seek to discover his will, neither of which might figure prominently in their scheme of things. Because we are nearer to the Israelite–Jewish ethical tradition ourselves, we are struck by the (undoubted) differences, rather than by the under-lying similarities.

To get the balance right, then, we need to say something like this. Once the OT is read critically, it is difficult to claim it as an unequivocal support for one type of Christian or Jewish ethics rather than another. It cannot, for example, be made to justify the whole system of medieval church law, or to show the way with complete clarity on debated issues of the present day such as abortion or contraception. But this does not mean that it is compatible with *just any* ethical system, that one could take the OT into one's system and at the same time adopt a Hindu or Shintoistic ethical code, or commit oneself to a life of complete hedonism. It is not easy to spell out what moral principles are compatible or incompatible with the general drift of the OT, but it is not impossible, at least in principle. Our sense that the moral stance of the OT is simply chaotic derives largely from the fact that it is so much a part of our common western heritage that we cannot stand far enough away to recognize the family likeness among its writings, and thus to see how markedly they differ, as a whole, from those of other major religious and ethical systems. And, if we are biblical critics, our detailed study of the OT will make us acutely aware of differences within it which, seen from outside, are actually comparatively minor. It is important to keep a sense of proportion.

It remains true that the moral principles on which the OT books are agreed are of a fairly high order of generality – indeed, mostly commonplaces for anyone brought up in traditional western morality. In many cases they are shared with the other Semitic religious systems of ancient and modern times. But a commonplace is not necessarily a banality, especially when we live in a society whose hold on the traditional moral system of the West is no longer so firm as it once was, and where rival views of ethics have become genuine options. It can still make sense, in such a context, to speak of 'the biblical tradition' on particular moral issues, however careful and scrupulous we need to be in recognizing variations within it.

### THE BASIS OF ETHICS

If we turn, finally, to the question of the basis of ethics, the idea of a general drift in the OT can once again come to our help. In section III it was suggested how varied the approaches to ethics were in ancient Israel: not even wholly non-religious, 'conventionalist' types of ethics can be excluded, and within the religious tradition of morality there are a number of different threads. But as it stands in its finished form, the OT undoubtedly sees God as the fountainhead of ethical obligation, as of everything else. It is not just, however, that the idea of ethics as straightforwardly 'obedience to God's commands' takes over from all the other ways in which God's relation to moral obligation is understood, but rather that the final form of the OT represents a subtle synthesis of a number of ways of understanding this obedience. The basic category for ethics in the OT is, indeed, 'law'; but law as a translation of the Hebrew *torah*, which is a term of much wider application than law in the sense it normally bears in English. When the whole Pentateuch or even the whole OT is referred to in Judaism as 'the Torah', what is meant is a system of ethical instruction that includes not only the idea that God is the lawgiver, but also that he is the source of all moral order in the world and a model of justice and truth that human beings should imitate.

The best way to approach the OT ethical system as 'Torah', is to remember that the purpose of the OT is not primarily to give information about morality — any more than it is to give information about theology, as we saw in Chapter 6 — but to provide materials that, when pondered and absorbed into the mind, will suggest the pattern or shape of a way of life lived in the presence of God. Though the OT *contains* laws or rules in our sense, it contains much else besides, and it cannot simply be equated with a set of rules. Readers are meant to be directed in obeying God's will and living in fellowship with him, not only by carrying out the detailed prescriptions of the laws (in the narrower sense), but also by reading the narratives — which do presuppose and help to establish a pattern of moral behaviour; by worshipping God with the help of the Psalms; and by meditating on sayings of sages and prophets. Thus, for the final form of the OT, practical moral conduct is inextricably linked with what we would probably call 'spirituality': it is a matter of a style of life, not just of particular rulings on 'moral issues'. 'Torah' is a system by which to live the whole of life in the presence of God, rather than a set of detailed regulations to cover every individual situation in which a moral ruling might be called for. Though this idea can, and sometimes did, lead to a minute attention to details of conduct such as Christians call 'legalism', the motive force behind it was a desire to bring the whole of life under the control of God's rule — to 'accept the yoke of the Kingdom of heaven', as rabbinic sources sometimes put it.

The reason why 'Torah' was able to develop this all-pervasive character has something to do with a fusion of the various approaches to the basis of ethics we discussed above. Torah is, first, the legislation delivered to Israel through Moses on Mount Sinai. But if we look at it more closely, we get a clear impression that this is not simply a matter of potentially arbitrary commandments that God gave simply because he chose to. The law affords an insight into the contours of God's own ideal will for his people and for all mankind. This was sometimes expressed in later Judaism by saying that this same law that Moses received existed already before the creation of the world, and served as the pattern or even as the tool God used when he made the world. As the pattern of God's intentions – the guiding principle of his own conduct as well as of the conduct of Israel – it is rather more like what we might call natural law in many ways. God has made the world in such a way that it exhibits a moral order; and this has the corollary, drawn explicitly in later Judaism but already essentially present in the OT, that God himself is in some sense bound by his own laws. Within the OT this conviction comes out most clearly not in the law-codes themselves, but in those texts that are concerned with what in modern theology is called 'theodicy'. By this is meant books that seek to vindicate the justice and goodness of God in the face of experiences or arguments that seem to call it in question. The historical books, and many of the prophets, work with a basic conviction, which they try to urge on their hearers or readers, that God is just, even on human terms – that he himself adheres to the same moral principles that he expects mankind to observe; that he is as just as they would like to believe he is. The discussion of Ezekiel 18 (see Chapter 5) has shown that God is there portrayed as having the same rules for himself and his own conduct as he has for judging the conduct of Israel: contrary to what the exiled community supposed, he cannot be accused of changing the rules to suit himself. Thus 'natural' and 'revealed' law are regarded as one and the same thing. But this is not a matter of mere theory or of definition. It is a conclusion won through a hard struggle with the facts of the nation's experience, a struggle duly recorded by the OT writers.

But this fusion of the first two types of approach to the basis of ethics has the effect of establishing the third of them. To do good, on such a view, is to imitate God, to do the things he would do if he were a human being. And what these things are can be read off in some measure from the things he *has* done, especially his acts of love and faithfulness towards Israel in the crucial early years of its existence – in the Exodus, the giving of the promised land, the establishment of the temple and the other sacred institutions. It is just for this reason that it is essential to record these events. The rules God requires Israel to observe can be seen to be congruent with his own character only if the events that show what that character is are also recounted. His purposes for the future, in which that character will continue to be consistently manifested, also need to be included in any full account of the basis of Torah; and so the historical books run off without a break into prophetic books that confirm for the reader that God will continue to be in the future as he has been in the past, true to the sorts of moral principle that he imposes on his worshippers. It might be said, then, that for the OT as we have it ethics is a matter of imitating the pattern of God's own actions, in salvation and in creation, because these spring from a pattern that always exists in his own mind and by which he governs the world with justice and mercy. Torah – in one aspect simply the law of Moses – is in another aspect the design according to which the world was created, and which makes sense of it; and by adhering to it human beings form part of God's plan and enjoy a kind of fellowship with him. Though he is transcendent and so beyond human grasp, he is nonetheless knowable, because he shares a kinship with human beings, and especially with Israelites; for those who observe Torah are, in a sense, the most fully human people, fully realizing the purpose for which they were made. In this sense ethics is not so much a system of obligations as a way of communion with God, which is a cause for joy: hence the lyrical quality, so puzzling to us who use 'law' in a much narrower sense, of such passages in praise of the law as Psalm 19 or Ecclesiasticus 24.23ff. And hence the existence of the text that has so often struck Christian readers as artificial, repetitive, and legalistic, but that could well serve as a complete statement in miniature of OT ethics and, indeed, of much OT theology – Psalm 119: one hundred and seventy-six verses in praise of the Torah.

NOTES

1  M. Buber, *Kampf um Israel* (Berlin, 1933), pp. 68ff. In English: 'Imitatio Dei', in *Mamre: Essays in Religion* (London, Oxford University, 1946; Westport, Greenwood, 1970).

2  See A.J. Gunneweg, *Understanding the Old Testament* (London, SCM, 1978; Philadelphia, Westminster, 1978), chapter 4.

## FURTHER READING

Barton, J., 'The Basis of Ethics in the Hebrew Bible', in *Ethics and Politics in the Hebrew Bible* (ed. D.A. Knight), *Semeia* 66 (1995), pp. 11–22.

Barton, J., 'Understanding Old Testament Ethics', *Journal for the Study of the Old Testament* 9 (1978), pp. 44–64.

Birch, B.C., *Let Justice Roll Down: The Old Testament, Ethics, and Christian Life* (Louisville, Westminster/John Knox, 1991).

Janzen, W., *Old Testament Ethics: A Paradigmatic Approach* (Louisville, Westminster/John Knox, 1994).

Ogletree, T.W., *The Use of the Bible in Christian Ethics* (Oxford, Basil Blackwell, 1984).

Spohn, W.C., *What are they saying about Scripture and Ethics?* (New York, Paulist, 1983).

Wright, C.J.H., *Living as the People of God: The Relevance of Old Testament Ethics* (Leicester, Inter-Varsity Pess, 1983).

# 8

---

# The Old Testament and its Relationship to the New Testament

## PAUL JOYCE

How does the New Testament fit into the picture of the study of the Old Testament that the chapters of this book have presented? This is a very natural question, especially since the Old and New Testaments are nearly always found bound together as one book – or perhaps we should rather say that in Christian practice they are usually found together; this is a significant qualification, for it is important to realize that the question of the relationship between the Old and New Testaments is essentially a Christian issue. The very name 'Old Testament', used to define the Hebrew Scriptures, was coined by Christians to distinguish these writings from the literature of the early Church that began to be regarded as having authority. The relationship between these two bodies of literature may well interest the Jew or the historian of religions, but it is within the Christian tradition that the relationship between the two has been a burning issue. In fact the question of what Christians should do with the texts they had inherited from the ancient Israelites was the subject of lively debate from the earliest centuries of the Church.

We begin by reviewing the factors that have often raised problems for Christians when considering the place they should give to the Hebrew Scriptures. One factor has always been the apparent difficulty of the OT. So much seemed obscure and irrelevant. What was to be made of detailed rituals for sacrificial worship, or of long lists of names? How could one explain the glaring inconsistencies within many OT narratives (for example, David is introduced into Saul's court in 1 Sam. 16 as a man of war, but in the next chapter he is a peasant lad, unknown to Saul, who has never worn armour)? And what of the broader

Christian issue, the theological differences found within the OT (for example, between the generous openness to the nations of the world found in chapters 40–55 of Isaiah and the apparent very narrow nationalism of Ezra)? Another factor that affected attitudes to the OT within the Church was the very Jewishness of the Hebrew Scriptures. What relevance could these texts, produced by the ancient Israelites, possibly have for a Church that had broken away from its Jewish moorings? In the period of the early Church, one person in particular, named Marcion, argued for a total break with the Church's roots in Judaism, and in fact he rejected the OT altogether. In the 1930s, in Nazi Germany, anti-Jewish feeling put pressure on the Church to deny the authority of the OT. A further factor leading some to question the continued authority and relevance of the OT is the belief that the findings of modern science have contradicted the scientific views represented in the OT, and especially in the early chapters of Genesis.

We shall return to these questions, but we now turn to what is arguably the most important factor of all in the difficulties Christians experience when considering the place they should give to the OT: the existence of inconsistencies between the Old Testament and the New. The factors mentioned above all relate to general difficulties about the OT itself, but this factor is more crucial, involving as it does apparent conflict between the Testaments. Let us look at some examples. The alleged cruelty of parts of the OT has caused difficulty to many. A notorious case comes from Psalm 137, which begins with the words, 'By the waters of Babylon . . . '. In the final verse, the Psalmist says to Babylon, the nation that had exiled many of the people of Judah,

Happy shall he be who takes your little ones and dashes them against the rock!

How can this be squared with Jesus' saying in the Sermon on the Mount, 'If anyone strikes you on the right cheek, turn to him the other also'? Such difficulties occur not only with regard to human attitudes and behaviour, but also with regard to the picture presented of God. In 2 Samuel 6, we read of poor Uzzah, who touched the ark of the covenant to prevent it falling over as it was being carried to Jerusalem. Uzzah was only trying to be helpful, but he was struck dead by God for daring to touch the sacred object. Such incidents are not common in the OT, but how does the God who appears in them relate to the loving God whom the New Testament encourages Christians to call 'Abba'? Marcion, whom we mentioned earlier, took these questions so seriously that he actually claimed that the loving God of the NT was in fact a different God from the angry God of the OT! This may be a rather extreme response, but the problem is one that still worries many today.

Another contrast that has often been drawn between the Old Testament and the New relates quite closely to this. One of the central features of Paul's theology is his assertion that the law of the OT, which Israel was called upon to obey as the people of God, has been replaced in the gospel of Christ by the free gift of grace, or unmerited favour, given to all who believe in Christ. Much of Paul's language tends to stress the contrast between law and gospel rather strongly, but he was also aware of the important place of the OT in the Church. However, some other Christian theologians, since Paul's time, have stressed the contrast between law and gospel to such an extent that they have tended to set up a black and white dichotomy between the Old Testament and the New, with the OT representing a religion of oppression and legalism from which the NT frees us. Not surprisingly, on such a view the continued place of the OT as respected Scripture within the Church often tends to be questioned.

These then are some of the major factors that have raised problems for Christians when considering the place they should give to the Hebrew Scriptures. Let us now briefly look at some typical responses to these difficulties. These responses fall into two basic groups, namely those that in one way or another involve rejection of the OT, and those that affirm the importance of the OT for the Church.

The classic case of rejection of the OT within the Christian tradition is that of Marcion, about whom we should now say a little more. He was a very influential churchman of the second century, one of those who emphasized Paul's contrast between OT law and NT gospel to an extreme degree, so much so that he rejected the OT, which he regarded as speaking of a God other than the God who was Father of Jesus. This clearly placed him outside the ranks of orthodox Christians. The main factors leading Marcion to reject the OT seem to have been, primarily, the problem of inconsistencies between the Testaments, focusing especially on the apparently cruel aspects of the OT, and, secondarily (though for Marcion closely related to this primary factor), the very Jewishness of the OT. However, a significant fact to note at this point is that, in attempting to exclude the apparently cruel and the Jewish elements from the Bible, Marcion was unable to rest content with rejecting the OT. He also had to reject, as secondary additions, large sections of the NT where he found similar features.

Marcion's rejection of the OT was deliberate, and was part and parcel of his elaborate theological system. The form rejection of the OT takes today is generally very different, amounting usually to an embarrassed silence about that part of the Bible. This attitude, which might well be said to be typical of very many Christians, is rarely articulated clearly, but seems to derive from a number of the factors we mentioned earlier. Of particular importance here seem to be the supposed difficulty and obscurity of so much of the OT; the apparently cruel and primitive nature of large parts of it; and also the feeling that the OT is irrelevant to the modern world and even contradicts the scientific views of our age.

The alternative to rejecting or quietly ignoring the OT is to affirm its importance for the Church and to attempt to integrate it with one's understanding of the NT. This more positive response may take a wide range of forms. A common way of handling the OT in the early Church was to allegorize it. This approach recognized the difficulties presented by the OT, and sought to counter them by claiming that the real meaning of the OT was other than the plain sense of the text. For example, the Song of Songs, which is probably secular love poetry, was interpreted as referring to the relationship between Christ and his bride, the Church; or again, the apparently vindictive and cruel parts of a number of the Psalms (for example, Psalm 63, verses 9–10) were often understood to refer to the sinful tendencies within us – it was against these sinful tendencies and not against real human enemies that this violent language was directed. It cannot be denied that such methods often produced a very rich and edifying reading of the biblical text, but nevertheless it is hard to be satisfied with an interpretation of the OT that fails to do justice to the plain sense of the text, and few today support this allegorical approach as being the best way to understand the OT.

Much more common in the Church today is what is often called the fundamentalist approach to the Bible.[1] Like the allegorical approach, it attributes a high degree of authority to the OT, but differs in that it generally involves reading the biblical text in a very literal way. It is not unfair to say that, for the most part, this approach tends to ignore the difficulties we considered at the start of this chapter. Inconsistencies are generally harmonized, the differences between various parts or within certain sections of the OT are played down or explained as far as possible, and what cannot be explained is taken on trust as divinely inspired. The harsh elements of the picture of God's activity in the OT are taken very seriously, often resulting in a Christian theology in which the aspect of divine judgement looms large. The scientific views of the reader are generally made to conform to what are supposed to be the scientific truths of the biblical text or, alternatively, an attempt is made, however tortuously, to read the biblical text in a way that fits modern scientific theories. Particularly in the United States, dispensational theories (see Chapter 1, p. 22) solve some of the difficulties by claiming that parts of the OT refer only to God's purposes for the Jews, and have nothing to do with the Church.

There is no intention here to mock the fundamentalist position. It is sincerely held by large numbers of Christians in the world today. However, it will be suggested in this chapter that there can be no satisfactory way of reading the OT from a Christian standpoint unless the issues considered at the start of the chapter are at least taken seriously as issues. We shall suggest that those problems are by no means insuperable obstacles to a positive reading of the OT, and that intellectual honesty demands that they be recognized and confronted.

An approach that faces up to these questions head on, and yet provides the means whereby the OT with all its riches may be accorded a positive place within the Church, would seem to be what is needed. Let us consider how such an approach might tackle the problems we considered at the start of the chapter.

The early chapters of this book introduced the reader to the tools that have been basic to OT study for most of the past hundreds years, namely the methods of historical criticism. The use of the word 'criticism' here should not cause anxiety. The word is not used in its negative sense, suggesting an approach that picks holes in the Bible; the word refers rather to the application of rational thought to the understanding of the biblical texts, asking questions about the various literary forms they take, and seeing them against their historical backgrounds. Such historical criticism has, of course, been richly supplemented by newer approaches over recent decades; but the older critical methods did much to aid reflection on the relationship of the Old Testament to the New. We noted earlier that the sheer difficulty and apparent obscurity of much of the OT has often been an important factor in threatening the place of the OT in the Church. Historical criticism has shed a vast amount of light on these problems. For example, various inconsistencies or repetitions have in many cases been explained in terms of there being several different literary strands present. The inconsistencies in the story of David's introduction to Saul have often been explained in this way.[2] Legislation for sacrifice and lists of family descent have become easier to understand when seen against their historical background in the life of Israel, as this has been illuminated by careful study of the biblical texts and the literature of neighbouring cultures. Divergent attitudes, for example, to the place of non-Jews in God's plan, begin to make sense when seen as representing the perspectives of different periods, or at least different groups within Israel. Furthermore, this approach to the OT tends to understand passages such as those in Genesis about the creation of the world and of humankind to have been written for literary and theological purposes, attempting to express the relationship between God, the world and humanity. They need not be seen as scientific texts advancing rival views to those of modern science. It should not be thought for a moment that all the problems presented by the OT were solved by historical criticism; far from it – many questions remain unanswered, and scholars differ in their views about many issues. Nevertheless, a great deal has been discovered. Thanks to the application of historical criticism, the OT is no longer a closed book, and its alleged obscurity need no longer be an obstacle to its having a positive place in the Church. Moreover, the clarification of much of the obscurity of the OT has removed what was the major taking-off point for the allegorical approach. When sense can be made of the text as it stands, there is no need for elaborate allegory.

However, even where we feel we understand the OT better now, there are times when we are acutely aware of differences and inconsistencies between the Old Testament and the New. We suggested earlier that this is really the crucial issue in the debate over the place of the OT in the Church. What are we to make of Psalms that seem cruel and vindictive? Is not the harsh legalism of the OT incompatible with the gospel of love and grace we find in the NT? Here too a way forward has been provided by the application of historical criticism to the biblical texts. We have learned to recognize within both Old and New Testaments a rich diversity of theological standpoints, which has shown that it is quite inappropriate to think in terms of a sharp dichotomy or absolute contrast between the two Testaments. It is not true that the whole of the OT is cruel and vindictive; nor is it true that the NT is entirely without material that can seem harsh, rigorous, even primitive. Let us consider some examples.

It is certainly true that the last verse of Psalm 137 hopes to see Babylonian children dashed against the rocks, but it would be wrong to think of such a violent attitude as typical of the whole OT. In Leviticus 19.18 we read the familiar words, 'You shall love your neighbour as yourself'. In verses 33–4 of the same chapter this command is extended to enjoin similar behaviour towards any stranger resident among the Israelites. Furthermore, on a still broader scale there is a strong universalist tradition running through the OT (found for example in chapters 40–55 of Isaiah and in the books of Jonah and Ruth), a tradition that seems to look to the incorporation of foreign nations into the saving plans of the God of Israel. Turning to the NT, it is of course true that love and forgiveness are the dominant themes, but we cannot overlook the element of rigorous judgement, as described, for example, in chapter 25 of Matthew's Gospel. In the parable of the talents, the servant who failed to make good use of the money entrusted to him by his master is cast into 'the outer darkness, where there will be weeping and gnashing of teeth'. A few verses later, in a description of the final judgement, the wicked are told, 'Depart from me, you cursed, into eternal fire'. Thus the OT does not have a monopoly on such stern language. Such material may be difficult for us to relate to today, but if this is so, it is a problem presented by the New Testament as well as the Old.

We shall have to return to this issue, but first let us consider a further implication of recognizing the rich diversity of both Testaments. We mentioned earlier the tendency in some Christian theology to draw a strong contrast between, on the one hand, the OT emphasis on law and on obedience as the condition of divine favour and, on the other hand, the NT gospel of free and undeserved grace, with divine favour bestowed independently of any demand. Such a dichotomy is, however, quite unjustified, because both Old and New Testaments each contain much material stressing God's demands on his people, and also much material stressing his forgiveness and his gracious favour towards his people. For example, within the OT there is certainly a good deal of emphasis on the need for obedience to God's law, and on the penalties that will follow sin. But there is also material, such as that found in Ezekiel 36.26–7, where God promises to give Israel a new heart and a new spirit and so enable Israel to respond to him. Again, in Jeremiah 31.31–4 God promises to write his law on Israel's heart so that she will obey it, and gives an assurance that sin and iniquity will be forgiven. When we turn to the NT, Paul's emphasis on God's favour as free grace dependent on no human action is certainly very important, but the diversity of the NT also finds room for the Epistle of James, which stresses the need for faith to be expressed in good deeds. There can then be no absolute dichotomy between OT law and NT gospel. The tension between demand and grace is vital to both Testaments. The distinctive feature of the NT is rather that these themes are related to the person and work of Jesus Christ; just how this distinctive feature of the NT relates to the OT is a central question to which we shall return shortly.

We have suggested, then, that the OT does not have a monopoly on language that may strike us as harsh, rigorous, even occasionally primitive. We have argued that both Old and New Testaments contain a broad range of theology and language, which in both cases includes at times that which may seem to us stern and difficult. And so we have concluded that there can, as far as these issues are concerned, be no contrast between the Old Testament and the New, on the basis of which the place of the OT in the Christian Bible might be denied or at least seriously questioned. However, while we may have demonstrated that the major problems often raised with regard to the Old Testament apply also to the New, we have not escaped these problems, which are now seen to be relevant to the Bible as a whole. What do we make of the harsh and rigorous language we find in both Testaments? And how can we account for the presence in both Testaments of a variety of theological viewpoints?

The key to progress in understanding these problems lies in a clarification of what we mean by the authority of the Bible. In what sense is the Bible valid and true? It seems that we need a way of understanding the authority of the Bible that can find room for a rich diversity in the biblical witness, a diversity that can include (even, we suggest, in the NT) elements we may regard as relatively primitive. We should not imagine that the only way of viewing the authority of the Bible is one that assumes that texts must be either absolutely authoritative, in the sense of being timelessly infallible, or else completely without authority. Nor should we assume that the whole of the Bible (or the whole of each Testament) must, if regarded as authoritative at all, be thought of as uniformly authoritative, with every part as important or permanently valid as the next.[3]

Both the Old Testament and the New Testament are firmly rooted in history – this is part of their strength. Each was produced in a whole range of cultural settings, addressing the issues of those contexts, being influenced by or reacting against the ideas of those times. In this process, literature was produced that reflects the encounter of God with his people, and this encounter is often reflected so profoundly (in the Old Testament as well as the New) that today, many centuries later, much of this literature confronts us with great power. The biblical literature gains much of its authenticity and relevance to our times from its very rootedness in the real world of affairs in which it took shape. However, this very rootedness in culture means that the Bible cannot be regarded as authoritative in an absolute sense that fails to recognize its historically conditioned nature. Nor can it be regarded as authoritative in a uniform way. Because the biblical literature inevitably took shape amid the swirling mass of events and ideas that make up human history, it will at different points reflect the encounter of God with his people with varying degrees of profundity and insight. Moreover, since our own cultural setting is so different from the various settings in which the Bible was formed, it is not surprising that certain parts of the biblical witness will prove helpful to us, or 'ring bells' for us, more than others.

There will be parts of both Old and New Testaments that we shall not find very edifying or relevant, parts that seem particularly tied to the narrow concerns of their own day – for example, the vindictive ending of Psalm 137 or, perhaps, some of Paul's remarks about women or slaves. We would be foolish, however, to reject the whole of the Bible for this reason, with its wealth of profound religious truth. Why do so simply because the authority we ascribe to it cannot be an absolute or uniform authority? On the understanding of the authority of the Bible that we are proposing, a diversity in the biblical witness (including at times elements that seem to us relatively primitive) is quite acceptable. And once we recognize this diversity in both Testaments, there can no longer be a black and white dichotomy between the Old and New Testaments. The Old Testament, like the New, is valued and treasured for the riches it contains.

We have seen a number of ways in which the application of historical criticism has clarified and eased some of the problems associated with the relationship between the Old and New Testaments. But if historical criticism has eased many problems in this area, it has, in a sense, also raised one. Careful study of the biblical texts by these methods has made very clear the important differences that often exist between the probable original meaning of certain Old Testament material and the re-use of that same material in the New Testament. We must now address this question of the use of the Old Testament in the New Testament.

The New Testament uses Old Testament material in a wide variety of ways, but we shall here consider just a few characteristic examples. Sometimes it is stated very explicitly that the Old Testament is being quoted so as to show that the events recorded in the New Testament fulfil the promises of the Old. So, for example, we often find in Matthew's Gospel the formula, 'This happened to fulfil that which was spoken by the prophet . . .'. Some cases of the use of such a formula seem to relate Old Testament words to New Testament events in a very profound way. For example, at Matthew 2.15 the words of Hosea 11.1, 'Out of Egypt have I called my son', are quoted in connection with the sojourn of Jesus' family in Egypt. The words are used in Hosea of Israel coming out of Egypt in the Exodus, and the parallel with Jesus as representative of the new Israel is pleasing and profound. Some other cases of the use of this formula in Matthew are, however, less satisfying. At Matthew 1.22–3, the words of Isaiah 7.14, which speak of the birth of a child called Immanuel, are quoted in connection with the virgin birth of Jesus. Unfortunately, in the original Hebrew of Isaiah 7.14, while there is reference to the birth of a significant child to a young woman, there is no reference to a virgin birth. It is possible, however, to understand the Greek translation of Isaiah 7.14 to refer to a virgin birth, and it seems to be this that Matthew had in mind. We cannot help but feel less than fully convinced by such a case of 'fulfilment', which rests on the wording of a translation rather than on that of the original Hebrew of the OT.

In some other cases, the notion that the events of the New Testament fulfil the words of the Old is implicit rather than explicit. However, such cases are very similar to the more explicit formula we have just considered; they too look at the OT through Christian eyes, drawing freely on OT material to illuminate such questions as that of the status of Christ. Thus, for example, in Mark 12.35–7 Jesus is portrayed as quoting Psalm 110.1 in his debate with the scribes over whether it is appropriate to speak of the Christ (the Messiah) as the Son of David. Jesus says that in Psalm 110, David, the author of the Psalm, uses the phrase 'my Lord' when speaking of the Christ. Therefore since the Christ must be greater than David, the phrase Son of David is inadequate to describe the Christ. This provides a good example of the way the application of historical criticism to the Old Testament has shown us how far the New Testament understanding of material can diverge from its probable original meaning in the OT. It is now generally accepted that the Psalms were, for the most part, not written by David but rather were pieces composed later for use in the liturgy of the temple. This particular Psalm is usually thought to be from the ceremony of a royal coronation. It would probably be a temple official who would say the words, 'The Lord [that is, God] says to my Lord [that is, the new king of the line of David], "Sit at my right hand".' The way the Psalm is understood in the NT is very different from this. 'My Lord' is understood to refer not to an ordinary Davidic king but to the Christ. This in itself is not an altogether inappropriate extension of the meaning of the Psalm, for the hoped-for Christ or Messiah was to be a great king of the Davidic line. However, the whole point of Jesus' argument as represented in Mark's Gospel (that David called the Christ 'my Lord') depends on David having written this Psalm, whereas OT scholars are almost unanimous in the view that he very probably did not.

The problem that confronts us is this. How should we respond to such cases in which the New Testament seems to understand the Old in ways that diverge from the most likely original meaning? To begin with, we must recognize that many such cases do exist. Although we cannot by any means always be sure that we know what the original authors had in mind, historical criticism has enabled us in large part to discern where New Testament use of material diverges from the probable original meaning in the Old Testament. The New Testament generally

142

attempts to make sense for its own day of the words of the Old Testament; this inevitably leads to divergences, because the backgrounds and concerns of the Old and New Testaments are so very different. In contrast to the practice of the NT authors, modern biblical scholars applying the methods of historical criticism make a deliberate attempt to discover, however incompletely this must be, what sense the OT was intended to make for its own day. We must have the courage to acknowledge the differences between Old Testament meanings and New Testament interpretations, where such divergences exist; nothing is to be gained from artificial attempts to harmonize differences of this kind. The OT must be allowed to be itself: it is not merely resource material for Christian theology; it is not simply a 'preparation for the gospel', to use a phrase often applied to it in the Christian tradition. The OT represents theology in its own right, in the way it speaks about God, the world and humanity, addressing the issues and wrestling with the problems of OT times. The New Testament cannot be used as an absolutely normative key to the Old Testament. As we saw earlier, the NT is the product of a particular historical period, and naturally reflects and reacts to the concerns of that age. (The treatment of Psalm 110 in St Mark's Gospel is typical of first-century Jewish exegesis of the Scriptures.) Truth cannot be conveyed in a cultural vacuum. As we have said, this should not be a cause of anxiety: it is inevitably true of all literature and does not prevent us from ascribing a very high degree of authority to the NT writings. It does, however, mean that the NT cannot be used as a definitive key to the literature of other ages.

Up to this point we have approached the question of the use of the Old Testament in the New Testament in the light of the methods of historical criticism that have dominated biblical studies for most of the past two hundred years. The highlighting of the differences between the likely original meaning of Old Testament material on the one hand, and the use made of it in the New Testament on the other (with a strong emphasis on the primary importance of the original setting), is very typical of this 'historical–critical' approach. However, one of the newer methods introduced in Chapter 2 has some interesting light to shed on the matter of the use of the Old Testament in the New. In mind here is the wide influence of the insights of English and other modern literature studies, a phenomenon that often goes under the name of 'literary approaches' to biblical studies.

People involved in this kind of work have reflected a good deal on the way texts are read. Many great texts, secular 'classics' as well as religious scriptures, are of course handed on for centuries and read in many different situations. When texts are read in new contexts, new understandings may well emerge. We have come to understand the seemingly infinite potential that texts (especially poetic texts, but those in prose too) have to generate new insights in new circumstances. There is a growing recognition that meaning does not reside in some absolute way in the text alone, but emerges in the encounter between text and reader – and that the reader, whether individually or as part of a community, brings a great deal to the process of interpretation.

Not surprisingly, many have found help here in reflecting on the use of the Old Testament in the New. One effect of such literary insights has been that there is less of a tendency nowadays to disparage later uses of early material simply because they do not tally with what scholars take to be the probable original meaning. For example, a more positive assessment of Matthew's use of the Immanuel material from Isaiah is possible when it is seen in terms of the discovery of new possibilities within a rich and evocative text. Such developments have helped us understand more about how scripture functions in an on-going religious tradition, and have also enabled, at least for some people, a reintegration of certain features of pre-modern reading of scripture, features very familiar to the fathers of the early church and the scholars of the middle ages. For example, a literary approach that helps us envisage the discovery of new meanings in old texts can go together surprisingly well with traditional Christian talk of the Holy Spirit inspiring the reader of scripture and leading the Church into ever new truths. Such traditional language and the newer insights borrowed from literary studies have in common the conviction that the original writing down of words represents not the end but rather the beginning of an exciting story.

How then might we express the relationship between the Old Testament and the New in a positive way? The relationship can be thought of as consisting essentially in a great continuity of religious tradition. What we call the OT was the Bible of Jesus and of Paul. When Marcion, in the second century, sought to exclude the Jewish elements from the Bible, he could not rest content with rejecting the OT. He had, as we have seen, to reject large parts of the NT as well. In fact, if he had been absolutely consistent he would have had to reject the whole of the NT, for there is virtually nothing in it that does not owe a great deal to the OT and to the Judaism it shaped. The influence of Greek thought in the NT is not to be ignored, but it is overwhelmingly in terms of the categories and concepts of the OT that the New Testament authors express themselves. Broad theological concepts first grasped by the theologians of Israel later provided the framework of NT thought. Take, for example, the notion of a just and loving God who acts faithfully for his people, and the notions of sin and forgiveness – it is very much from the OT tradition that Christianity has inherited these and other basic categories. More specifically, the NT writers draw on certain key phrases or even institutions of the OT in their attempt to make sense of Jesus' life and death. Titles or phrases such as 'Son of Man', 'Servant' and 'Messiah' (the Hebrew word of which the Greek word 'Christ' is a translation) are reapplied to Jesus in the difficult task of trying to express his significance. The meanings of these originally distinct and separate OT titles or phrases are often modified considerably in the process of being brought together and reapplied to Jesus, but their origin is unmistakably in the OT. In a similar way, the ideas associated with the important Old Testament institution of temple sacrifice are employed in the New Testament (for example, in the Epistle to the Hebrews) in the attempt to make some sense of Jesus' terrible death.

Thus it was very largely the OT that provided the theological vocabulary the authors of the NT used to express their insights into God's activity in Jesus. These authors had a strong sense of their continuity with OT tradition, and so it can indeed be very helpful to think of the relationship between the Old Testament and the New Testament in terms of a great continuity of religious tradition. But on its own the language of continuity is insufficient. The New Testament writers speak of experiencing a distinctively new and decisive act of God in Jesus. The very names Christians give to the two parts of their Bible – Old Testament and New – signal that there is not only continuity but also an essential discontinuity. We have argued that some approaches that set up a sharp dichotomy between the Testaments have proved unhelpful, but this should not be taken to mean a denial of the radical newness claimed by the authors of the NT.

How are we to express this newness? One way is to speak of the New Testament as realizing the best hopes and aspirations of the

Old. Such talk of hopes being realized is certainly preferable to language about predictions being fulfilled, since to speak of prediction and fulfilment tends, as we have seen, to reduce the OT to a mere preparation for the Christian gospel, rather than a theology in its own right. But it is doubtful whether the language of hopes realized can on its own do full justice to the disjunction implied by the rather uncompromising claims of the NT, especially the claim that Jews who did not affirm Jesus as Messiah would thereby exclude themselves from salvation. The distinctive, particular claims of Christianity need to be taken with full seriousness and not watered down in the interests of finding an easy answer to the question of the relationship between the Testaments.

But if it is vital to take the particularity of the Christian tradition seriously, then we have also to be aware that the OT is still read by another very distinctive tradition, namely the ongoing tradition of Judaism.[4] If some earlier generations of Christians could quietly ignore this, we today cannot, living as we do in a period of history that has seen both the shameful horrors of the Holocaust and also the remarkable re-establishment of Israel as a nation state. As we reflect on these two religious communities, both of which today read the OT, we should also bear in mind two important issues about terminology. First, a term best avoided is 'the Judaeo–Christian tradition', since it tends to lump Judaism and Christianity together in a rather indiscriminate way and, worse, often implies a swallowing up of the Jewish tradition within Christianity. Second, because of a strong awareness that the OT is read also by Jews, many people today prefer to avoid altogether the term Old Testament (which is of course not used by Jews), and to employ instead the less contentious term Hebrew Bible. While the continued use of 'Old Testament' is justified within specifically Christian settings (including, of course, Christian discussion of the relationship between the Testaments), 'Hebrew Bible' is often a helpful way of avoiding begging major theological questions when the context of debate is other than specifically Christian.[5]

We acknowledged at the start of this chapter that the issue of the relationship between the Testaments is distinctively a Christian one. Indeed, this discussion inevitably throws up major questions about the nature of Christianity and its relationship to Judaism. To read the scripts of ancient Israel as 'Old Testament' is to read them *as* a Christian. But if we take the modern reality of Judaism as a living faith seriously (rather than dismiss it as a dead religion that should have withered away centuries ago), how can we make sense of the fact that the same ancient scriptures are read so differently in these two traditions? Perhaps we can learn here from the literary approaches we mentioned earlier: we should speak of Judaism and Christianity as two ongoing reading communities, two contexts of interpretation. This would offer a way of taking each tradition with full seriousness. The scriptures inherited from ancient Israel – Isaiah, the Psalms and the rest – are naturally and appropriately read very differently within each of these two distinct reading communities, and the rules governing such reading are primarily those of coherence with community norms. In other words, how you read depends on within which community you read, Jewish or Christian. To approach things in this way need not imply the abandonment of the idea of ultimate truth or a slide into sheer relativism; one is indeed called to make judgements between religious options, to strive to discriminate between sense and nonsense as best one can. But it does, as we have said, imply the recognition that to read the scriptures of ancient Israel as 'Old Testament', within the context of the Christian Bible, is to read them as a Christian. The distinct Jewish and Christian approaches to the shared text are part and parcel of the two distinct 'worlds of meaning' represented by Judaism and Christianity respectively. Each of these worlds of meaning can only be fully appreciated from within, and though we must each be as true as possible to our vision of the truth, judgements between these visions must in the last resort rest with God.[6]

### NOTES

1  See J. Barr, *Fundamentalism* (2nd edn, London, SCM, 1981).
2  It should be acknowledged that in recent years many have begun to question the adequacy of such theories of different strands. This is particularly true of those most influenced by the newer literary approaches, who generally try to understand the text, with all its tensions, in the form in which it has come to us. See, for example, D.M. Gunn and D.N. Fewell, *Narrative in the Hebrew Bible*, The Oxford Bible Series (Oxford, OUP, 1993).
3  A subtle exploration of the theme of biblical authority may be found in J. Barton, *People of the Book? The Authority of the Bible in Christianity* (London, SPCK, 1988).
4  For the purposes of this discussion we leave to one side Islam, within which the OT has a place of honour.

5 For a lively discussion of the use of the terms Old Testament and Hebrew Bible, a pair of articles in the journal *Theology* must be consulted: J.F.A. Sawyer, 'Combating Prejudices about the Bible and Judaism' (July/August 1991, pp. 269–78); R.W.L. Moberly, ' "Old Testament" and "New Testament": The Propriety of the Terms for Christian Theology' (January/February 1992, pp. 26–32).

6 For a fuller expression of the position adopted at the end of this chapter, see P.M. Joyce, 'A Tale of Two Sisters: Judaism and Christianity', in *Theology* (September/October 1993), pp. 384–90.

# 9

---

# Epilogue –
# Using the Old Testament

## JOHN ROGERSON

Many who study the Old Testament do not wish to be content with knowing about it from the literary and historical–critical point of view. They wish to use it in their lives. For those who become full-time workers in the Church, there may be the necessity to preach about the OT or to lead discussion groups on OT books or themes. Those who enter the teaching profession may be expected to know about the ways in which the OT can be applied to social and moral questions.

College and university courses that include the study of the OT often do not cover these matters. Many regard it as the task of theological seminaries to teach such things. There is sometimes a gulf between what is taught academically about the OT and the use professional people are expected to make of the OT. Several of the essays in this book have pointed to some of the ways in which the academic foundations for the modern use of the OT can be laid. This Epilogue seeks to address itself more directly to the subject of using the OT.

## *Using the Old Testament in the Church*

In church services the Old Testament is usually required to play a secondary role to the New Testament. Whereas books of the NT may be read and preached upon systematically, OT readings are usually chosen because they are thought to illumine or to anticipate the NT readings. An effect of this is that many congregations are not familiar with the OT as a whole, but are fed a diet of readings gleaned from all over the OT, and have very little idea how these are related. Apart from the chapters of

Genesis that deal with creation and 'fall', there may be few passages of the OT that become the subjects of sermons in their own right. References to the OT may often assert what earlier sections of this book have sought to deny – for example, that the OT presents a God of wrath while the NT presents a God of love, or that the OT is simply a record of religious evolution from primitive and barbaric conceptions of God to something approaching the spirit of the Sermon on the Mount.

One fact that has been constantly stressed in previous chapters is that of *diversity* within the OT. It is precisely this diversity that should be the starting point for the use of the OT in the Church. The fact is that the OT was produced over such a long period of time, and in so many different situations, that many circumstances of the religious life of the churches and of individuals today are inevitably paralleled in the OT. The OT is particularly candid about doubt and uncertainty, for example, and in parts of books such as Jeremiah, the Psalms, Job and Ecclesiastes it expresses sentiments that must occur to many sensitive Christians today.

At another level, because its historical traditions span such a long stretch of time, the OT enables us to get a perspective on the interrelationship between God's search for mankind and that confused response of his people that ranges from positive commitment to outright rebellion (via indifference and the desire to use God merely to further human ambitions). Because the story of God's search and the people's response covers so much time, it provides a warning against regarding any particular segment of the story as the whole truth. Elijah's complaint that he alone is left of all the servants of God, and that even his life is threatened (1 Kings 19.10), is as unrepresentative of the fortunes of the people of God as are those apparent high points of Israel's history in which zealous kings forced religious compliance upon a reluctant people. The narratives of the ups and downs of the fortunes of the people of God in the OT can help the Church today to set its life in a wider context of the call of God and the responses of the people. It can serve as a corrective to false prophets of doom or prosperity, who deduce from their immediate situations the imminent demise of the Church or the imminent conversion of the world.

One of the most fundamental problems of the Church today (by no means a new problem) is that of the inclusive versus the exclusive Church. This can be illumined by the OT. The problem is whether the Church should consist only of the totally committed, i.e. be exclusive, or whether it should embrace many members who may never be more than nominal Christians. The OT does not decide in favour of either alternative; rather, it exposes the shortcomings of both positions.

Basically, Israel as the people of God was something inclusive. Membership was a matter of birth, but the existence of the whole people depended upon the grace of God. God had shown that grace supremely in the Exodus deliverance, but also in subsequent dealings with the people. The response to this grace and to membership of the people of God was to be obedience to God's law and covenant (cf. the opening of the Decalogue: 'I am the LORD your God, who brought you out of the land of Egypt . . . you shall have no other gods before me' (Exodus 20.2–3)). In the event, the response fell short of what might have been expected. The people turned to other gods; when these failed them, they turned back to God, but forgot him as soon as their immediate problems were solved. Some of the most remarkable illustrations of this type of response are to be found in the traditions about the wilderness wanderings. Here, the very generation that had experienced the deliverance from Egypt behaved so faithlessly that it was condemned not to enter the promised land, a fate Moses was also forced to share (cf. Deut. 32.48–52).

The pitfalls of the inclusive view of the people of God are clear. By no means everybody is grateful for unsolicited inclusion in the people of God, with the attendant responsibilities. Unwilling and unco-operative members of the people of God can make life hard for those who are faithful, or for the chosen ministers of God. On the other hand, an inclusive view of the people of God asserts the lordship of God over every aspect of the life of the people, whether they like it or not. Religion is not an affair for the few who like that sort of thing. Religion is an important part of reality, and the faithful must be prepared to suffer on account of, and on behalf of, the unfaithful, as they maintain their vision.

The exclusive view of the people of God is represented, for example, by the post-exilic community in Jerusalem, from which were expelled all who were not of proper descent (e.g. Nehemiah 13.23–30). It is often said that the books of Jonah and Ruth, both of which describe the faith of non-Israelites, were written in protest at this exclusivism. Whatever may be the truth of this suggestion, both Ruth and Jonah maintain that the purposes and working of God cannot be confined to the chosen people, let alone to an idealized or exclusive form of the chosen people. An exclusive idea of the people of God may avoid the problem of the half- or non-committed, but it runs the risk of narrowing God's purposes until they concern only the people of God as narrowly defined.

Ancient Israel as the people of God, whether considered inclusively or exclusively, and the Church, share the situation that they owe their existence to divine grace in the past, and that they look forward to a consummation in the future. Just because OT hopes are in one sense fulfilled for Christians in the ministry, death and resurrection of Jesus, it must not be overlooked that the Church still looks for a consummation, and that the OT supplies many of the categories in which the NT describes that consummation. The effective acknowledgement by all the nations that God is king is no more complete for the Church than it was for ancient Israel. In spite of God's revelation in Jesus Christ, the Church is no more a willing dedicated instrument for his purposes than was Israel. Because ancient Israel and the Church both live in the paradox of the already and the not-yet, much material in the OT can provide illumination for church life.

At the level of the individual, the OT contains, especially in its Psalter, the repository of the inspiration, hopes, doubts and fears of generations of believers. In its insights into the heart of mankind, its terminology for wrongdoing is more profound and far-reaching than what is to be found in the NT (cf. Psalm 51). It would do no harm if preachers who speak glibly about 'sin' were to make a careful study of the vocabulary of the OT in the matter of wrongdoing and rebellion against God.

There are no simple hermeneutical rules that can be applied to the OT to make it yield messages for any conceivable situation today. Its use in the Church requires at least the following:

- knowledge of its whole content;
- a recognition of its diversity;
- a readiness to avoid over-simplifying formulae such as that it displays primarily a God of wrath;
- a willingness to see it as a witness to the faith of people who lived in real and often difficult circumstances;
- a readiness to learn all that is possible from academic and critical scholarship.

Ultimately, such is the diversity of the OT that its use in the Church will be to some extent a personal matter for each serious user. Different users will be drawn to different parts of it, and will apply those parts to their own particular circumstances. The work involved will be considerable, but so are the potential rewards for the Church.

## *Using the Old Testament in social and moral questions*

One of the current features of life in Britain is the rise of single-issue groups in the churches and the wider community. In some cases these groups have appealed to the OT for support. Within the churches, the issue of homosexual relationships and whether homosexuals should be ordained has sharply divided congregations. An issue that has united some churches and trades unions is that of Sunday trading, while concern for the environment has brought together church members, 'new age' believers, Green Party activists and young and old idealists. While the prominence accorded the OT by some of these groups is to be welcomed, few professional OT scholars will be happy with the way they use the Bible. The observations that follow are not intended to suggest that professional students of the Bible should have a veto on how others use it. The purpose is rather to enter a plea for a responsible use of the Bible.

Two issues, homosexuality and creation, will be addressed, but as a preliminary, some comments will be made on a matter on which the Bible teaches clearly, namely that it is wrong to lend and borrow money on interest. In Psalm 15, among the virtues expected of those who will dwell on God's holy hill are that they will not put out their money at interest (Psalm 15.5); and Deut. 23.19–20 explicitly forbids an Israelite to lend to another Israelite upon interest, although an Israelite may charge interest to a foreigner. In the early church it was held that Jesus' attitude to earthly possessions ruled out the taking of interest, and for at least twelve centuries it was the teaching of the churches that taking interest was wrong. As late as the end of the sixteenth century, in Shakespeare's *The Merchant of Venice*, the difference between the Christian merchant Antonio and the Jewish money lender Shylock was that the Christian refuses to charge interest. Modern audiences can find the anti-semitism of the play disturbing; but it would be interesting to know how many members of a modern audience are also disturbed by the assumption that Christian merchants do not charge interest.

The point of these observations about interest is that something upon which churches depend today for their income, and on which citizens in the west depend for their pensions or for buying houses, was for much of the history of the Church believed to be prohibited by the Bible. What this shows is that, whether we like it or not, it is difficult to establish and apply biblical principles to society. Furthermore, a study of the history of the use of the Bible indicates that such use has always been contextual, that is, shaped by changing attitudes in society at large. Thus the Bible is no longer used to justify slavery, capital punishment or the death penalty for stealing, in addition to which a number of things commanded in the OT, such as the following provisions in one brief passage (Deut. 21.15–22.24), are illegal in modern Britain: that a man with two wives (British law prohibits a man from having two wives) must make his first-born son his main heir even if this son was not born to the man's favourite wife; that citizens have the right to stone to death a stubborn and rebellious son; that birds' eggs may be taken from a nest but not the mother bird; that a bride who is found not to be a virgin on her wedding night is to be stoned to death; likewise a man and woman found committing adultery.

None of these instances can decide what the OT says about homosexuality, or whether or not that teaching should be applied today. What these instances (and the case of interest) show, however, is that using the Bible today is not simply a matter of reading texts and applying what they say. Further, when I discuss with people just such matters as the Bible's teaching on homosexuality, I am always interested to know why they may feel strongly about applying the Bible's teaching in this particular case, while not doing so in other cases – for example, those of not charging interest, or the stoning to death of brides who lost their virginity prior to marriage.

Discussions about homosexuality need to distinguish between homosexual orientation and homosexual acts. Once this distinction is made, it has to be recognized that the OT says nothing about homosexual orientation and, of course, nothing about lesbianism. Three passages are usually cited in discussion: Gen. 19, Judges 19 and Lev. 18.22 and 20.13. The first two passages can be dealt with quickly. If they refer to homosexual actions (this has been disputed), then these actions involve the actual or suggested communal sexual abuse in public of innocent victims. Presumably no reader of the Bible will think that such conduct is acceptable today. The passages in Lev. 18 and 20 condemn 'a man who lies with a male as with a woman', and prescribe the death penalty for such people.

The Leviticus texts occur in longer passages that prohibit sexual relationships within the immediate family. As such, they no doubt express the universal fear in societies of the consequences of incest. But they also state the minimum requirement for a group to survive: that its members marry outside the immediate family. From this perspective, intercourse between males does nothing to perpetuate the group, and is condemned. Our situation today is quite different. The survival of particular families is not vital for the survival of a community. We do not live in the small agricultural villages typical of ancient Israel, where the maintenance of the population in the face of disease and war was vital to the survival of the village. To pluck these texts out of their context and to apply them without remainder to today's world is not a responsible use of the Bible. To assert that these texts contribute to the question of whether or not homosexuals should be ordained is pure fantasy.

The fact is that many of the laws of the OT are directed to an agricultural peasant society that no longer exists in the industrialized west. Not only does this make laws such as those about fallowing fields, vineyards and olive orchards irrelevant; western society no longer has slaves, nor would it stone to death people who worked on the sabbath (cp. Num. 15.32–36). The statements about a man lying with a male as with a woman in Lev. 18 and 20 can no more be applied to today's western society than can the law that a city should stone to death a rebellious and stubborn son. Further, if the commandments in Lev. 18 and 20 *are* plucked from their context and applied to today's problems, this introduces a method of interpretation that diminishes the importance of the contribution that the Bible can make to today's problems. The principle that is introduced is that a text can be applied so long as it is acceptable to at least some body of opinion existing today in the west. But this approach is not only highly selective, it is hostage to the fact that in previous centuries this very same approach defended and then had to abandon such things as slavery, the death penalty for stealing, and the wrongness of a man marrying his deceased wife's sister.

A more responsible way of using the OT is by way of imperatives of redemption and structures of grace. An imperative of redemption is a call to Israelites to act graciously because God has been gracious to them. A structure of grace is an administrative arrangement or strategy for action that seeks to achieve graciousness in practical terms. In Ex. 23.9–12 an imperative of redemption is cited in the commandment –

> You shall not oppress a stranger; you know the heart of a stranger, for you were strangers in the land of Egypt.

The Israelites' experience of being oppressed and the implied fact that they have been delivered is the ground for the command to be gracious to foreigners who take refuge with them.

The passage then goes on to specify further structures of grace. Land, vineyards and olive orchards are to be fallowed every seventh year, and anything that they produce must be left for the poor and for the wild animals. Since it was necessary to fallow fields every second or third year in ancient Israel, while vineyards and olive orchards did not need to be fallowed at all, this is not an agricultural necessity made into a theological virtue. It is an attempt to create a structure of grace in which fields and their trees and, derivatively, the poor and wild animals will enjoy rest because God gave rest to the Israelite slaves in Egypt when he delivered them. A narrative about divine graciousness is meant to shape the social and natural order. The same is true of the continuation of the passage where the sabbath-day law is restated with the first beneficiaries being an owner's ox and ass, domesticated animals that could easily be worked non-stop.

If OT laws are approached in the way just outlined, if they are seen as attempts within their particular setting to order life graciously so as to reflect the graciousness of God, they obtain an immediacy denied by the selective approach criticized above. They challenge us by their example to ask what the imperatives of redemption may be that are relevant to our world, and they invite us to work out appropriate structures of grace for our situations. In this, they challenge our sensitivity, our imagination and our creativity in the way that the words 'Go and do thou likewise' do at the end of the parable of the Good Samaritan.

These observations lead to brief comments about creation. The OT, by contrasting the vegetarian world of Gen. 1.29–30 with the flesh-eating world of Gen. 9.2–4, declares that the world of Gen. 1 is not the world of our experience. The world of our experience is a world not at peace with itself, and the OT looks forward in several passages to a new creation in which the violence imminent in the world will be removed. 'The wolf and the lamb shall feed together, the lion shall eat straw like the ox' (Is. 65.25). Given this view, it is not surprising that the OT neither envisages nor practises a 'creation spirituality' that seeks to imitate the world of nature. Israel's neighbours who did imitate nature practised sacred prostitution and translated into social terms the principle in nature that the strong should dominate the weak. The OT wishes the natural world, as much as the social world, to be shaped by narratives that are grounded in the gracious actions of a God who sets people free.

# Index